MEANDER BELT

AMERICAN LIVES

Series editor: Tobias Wolff

MEANDER
BELT

Family, Loss, and
Coming of Age in the
Working-Class South

M. Randal O'Wain

UNIVERSITY OF NEBRASKA PRESS | *Lincoln*

Library of Congress Cataloging-in-Publication Data
Names: O'Wain, M. Randal, author.
Title: Meander belt: family, loss, and coming of age
in the working-class South / M. Randal O'Wain.
Description: Lincoln: University of Nebraska
Press, [2019] | Series: American lives
Identifiers: LCCN 2019005283
ISBN 9781496213310 (paperback: alk. paper)
ISBN 9781496217271 (epub)
ISBN 9781496217288 (mobi)
ISBN 9781496217295 (pdf)
Subjects: LCSH: O'Wain, M. Randal. | O'Wain, M. Randal—
Family. | Fathers and sons—United States—Biography. |
Authors, American—Southern States—Biography.
Classification: LCC PS3615.W26 Z46 2019 |
DDC 814/.6 [B]—dc23 LC record available
at https://lccn.loc.gov/2019005283

Set in New Baskerville ITC by E. Cuddy.
Designed by N. Putens.

To Mesha Maren for her love and support

To the living: my mother, my sisters,

and my nephews and nieces

and

To the dead: my father, Chris,

and my brother, Christopher

I walked up the steps and stood on the porch
A woman I didn't recognize came and spoke to me
through a chained door
I told her my story and who I'd come for
She said "I'm sorry son but no one by that name
lives here anymore."

BRUCE SPRINGSTEEN, "My Father's House"

CONTENTS

PREFACE

Memory is often inaccurate. Years pass, and within these years, new stories meld with formative experiences. Life events, such as grief over the loss of a parent and sibling, alter the positioning of light within memory. I have written in a style most natural to me as an artist, one that mirrors fiction, in a sense, and this, too, complicates the accuracy of memory. I am not, nor have I ever been, much interested in accuracy. I'm interested in verisimilitude. Accuracy is irrefutable fact and does not allow for the messy and difficult emotions that persist within memory; verisimilitude is the essence of what is true to the human heart. That said, I enjoy constraints. I have refused to collapse my loved ones into composite characters, and I have not knowingly adjusted time lines. I have, however, reconstructed my narrative by using sensory details, description, dialogue, and action. I have changed the names of people because we live in a hypernosey culture with access through social media. I have also omitted people in order to create a more concise and elegant narrative.

MEANDER BELT

I   Mirrored Mezzanine

With the covers drawn to my neck, I count cars that pass on Young Avenue, worrying over my father's absence from dinner. Perhaps because he missed a few meals in a row, or maybe my concern stems from the rain that has fallen all day and night. Outside my window, I hear the *ssshiinnggs* of tires against wet asphalt but no engine sounds like his truck. *I'll wait for him*—but soon I fall asleep, and a hungry fear wakes me seconds before I feel his heavy hand shake my shoulders. I play with this jolt as I zero in on my father's face crouched close to mine. He is dressed in a thin jean jacket with fur around the collar, a pair of aviator shades holding back a loose mane of long hair—"Come on," he says. "I want to show you something." I do not trust the urgency in his voice, cannot understand why he needs to pull me from bed. I only calm when my older brother, Chris, appears in the doorway, a cool look of annoyance on his face.

On the way to the car, Chris moves as Dad does, chest puffed and shoulders squared, shuffling forward as if led by the button of his jeans. My father loads my younger sister, Amanda, into her booster. My mother smokes with the passenger window cracked. And then we drive, and I (not aloud, never aloud in front of my father) whine about the length of the car ride, about the uncertainty of our destination. He tells us that where we are going is a surprise.

A lone building, tall and narrow, made almost entirely of glass stands in the center of a massive lot, and my father parks just outside the double brass doors. He carries my sleeping sister from the car, her body draped over his torso, head resting in the crook of his neck. When he tosses his set of keys in the air, a bulbous mess of jangling sound, he laughs, catching them on the way down. I run to him, my face at the same level as the door handle, and watch as he fingers the ring in search of the corresponding key—gold, wrapped in a pink sticker, muddied with prints. He smiles when the lock clicks free. I know now the pleasures of pride; I can imagine the sense of accomplishment this sound must have provided my father, a thirty-year-old construction worker—keys mean trust, respect. Keys also mean home, and so I follow his hand with suspicion.

Once inside, we take the elevator up to an expansive room: seafoam walls, electric sockets uncovered, exposed entrails of capped-off wiring. Familiar objects are spread over a cloth tarp, objects I associate with my father—joint compound, troughs and spades, paper tape without adhesive, a cordless drill, and a tool belt.

It's this way, he says, waving us through a heavy wooden door and into an unfurnished restroom mezzanine where large mirrors cover the walls and floor and ceiling. There is a small window, and as the mirrors reflect off one another, the mezzanine is cast in silver. There is no up and no down until my family, crowding closely together, break the room open—I see myself below me, above me, beside me. My father puts his hand on my shoulder and pushes me toward one wall, my brother on his other side, Amanda asleep in his arms. He tells us how to look, kneeling next to Chris and pointing to the reflections behind his reflection. See? Their bodies repeat ad infinitum, dressed identically, grinning into the smallest images of themselves. I count the reproductions, first the front and then the back—long hair hanging past each of their shoulders, blue eyes too large in each of their faces—until I cannot see their eyes, can't make out their sharp jawlines. My excitement inverts, turns to panic. These are faces and bodies so like the ones known to me but distant, perhaps stolen in the last capture. I shake my head, focusing again on the *me* just beyond my ear, so close to the mirror my breath draws fog, but I am confused to find only the back of my head—hair matted from sleep. My sister howls, a raspy, dry screaming that begins the moment she opens her eyes, surprised to be somewhere far from home. Patting her back, shushing, my parents leave the mezzanine together.

I lie down—at the tips of my fingers are further fingers. Above me I locate my disappearing twins, and I trace my likeness the way I had with my brother and father until I cannot recognize my face but only the contours of my head and my breathing grows shallow because I fear an end. I fear an end because it is a mystery, a phenomenon, the hundreds of replicas I narrate with no conclusion—he is me but different; he is not me but looks the same; he is me and is the same; he will go home and sleep and share my future; he will share the opposite future. My father was right. I love the surprise. My earlier unease is replaced by awe when, for the first time I can recall, I think of him as a man separate from provider, a man who built a room made of mirrors, a room that tilts the normal world into the extraordinary.

When he comes to fetch me, I ask him where the reflections end.

"They don't," he says.

11   Arrow of Light

The evening Jimmy died, my father ran late picking me up from
Webelos. I sat under a Japanese maple and practiced the square
knot, the last knot I needed to master before receiving my Arrow
of Light badge. Then I could enter Boy Scouts at ten, instead of
eleven. Useful for survival, the square knot works as a binding knot—
good for clamping a wound but not the best for carrying things or
securing them. I threaded one rope over another twice, made a
loop, and pulled. Grass and leaves make good wound compresses,
as long as they aren't poisonous like ivy or oak.

Behind me, tires squealed, and I turned to see my father's
beat-up green truck out front of the stone rectory.

"Come on," he yelled. "Hurry up." His hair hid most of his
face and twiggy autumn trees reflected in his aviator shades, but I
could still make out his expression, one that made us kids hide in
our rooms. "We got to check on Jimmy."

Jimmy was a familiar addition to family dinners. When he came
around, my parents laughed and talked loud. He threw my brother
and me over his shoulders and snuck us sips of beer. I often sat

between the two men in the truck cab on errands, each fragrant with car grease and sawdust as they smoked, Jimmy's tattooed arm hitched to the window, a canvas of black lines and fading color, my father's hair whipping in the wind. For a moment, I felt happy as I slipped into the truck, but he drove too fast, barely missing red lights, passing cars. "Drive, fucker!" he'd yell at a city bus or left-turning dump truck.

At Jimmy's house my father fishtailed into the driveway and threw the truck into park. "Don't let me catch you in the yard," he said.

I waited for him to go inside before I stepped out, found a low-hanging branch nearby, and practiced the square knot on the limb as if it were a fellow scout's bleeding arm.

After a few minutes, my father stormed out the front door with Deborah, Jimmy's wife, in tow. I crouched by the tree and heard her say, "Hurry up. Cops'll be here soon." My father didn't respond. He moved fast across the yard toward Jimmy's truck. I saw then the busted rear windshield.

After opening the passenger door, my father drew back quick and vomited. I'd never seen him sick before. He bent down low, holding his hair away from his face, and fought to catch his breath before throwing up a second time. Still begging for air, my father wiped his mouth on his flannel sleeve. For a moment, he stood motionless holding his arm against his mouth. Then he reached into the truck, dug around, and came out with a small but weighted plastic bag. He walked back toward Deborah. "Flush it," he said. Perhaps I saw white powder in the bag; perhaps I only see it in memory. I would later learn my father was called over to hide cocaine his friend had been snorting before he shot himself.

I unmade the square knot I'd just tied off, and I hid behind the tree. My father returned with a different bag, this time a ziplock. He reached into the driver's side where Jimmy lay. Years later, when I was twenty, he told me how he had gathered up viscera to bury privately. He relived this memory more than once during regular postmidnight phone calls to the dim, filthy house where I lived in Olympia, Washington. I recall his actions with admiration. In some primordial sense, his secreting away—even, or especially, in light of what I can only imagine to be wild shock—feels psychically familiar, as if I, too, would have done the same thing. When my father pulled away from the truck, I saw him stuff the bag into his pocket. He paused, briefly, before he reared back and kicked the side of Jimmy's truck—"Stupid motherfucker!" He kicked the door once more.

A police car came up the drive, without lights or sirens. My father walked toward the officer. Deborah came out of the house and stood a little ways off. This time, she held her infant son. "Y'all needed an ID," my father said to the cop and pointed toward Jimmy's truck. "Well, it's him." The cop took down my father's name in a little notebook. "Oldest friend," my father said to a question I couldn't hear. An ambulance arrived.

"Back in the truck," he told me.

On the drive home, he kept quiet, cigarette clamped tight between his teeth. He smoked without using his hands. "Should've just left you at the church," he said.

"No," I said. "I wanted to come."

We stopped at a red light. His face crumpled the way mine did when I tried not to cry. I stared down at my shirt, played with the yellow, red, and green tassels that hung from my Webelos badge. My father flicked his cigarette out the window. There were tears, but I pretended not to see. He turned on the radio—*Do-do-do. Looking out my back door*—and cranked up the volume.

No one talked to me about Jimmy after that day. My brother, Chris, and I didn't attend the public funeral held for him. Instead, our grandmother kept an eye on us. The familiar sounds and smells of frying chicken and steamed greens took over the house. My brother and I hid upstairs in our rooms. I stayed clear of Nana because any time our parents were away, she taped my ears against my head. "Keep 'em from sticking out so far."

I was bored playing alone, and I went down the hall to find my brother. In an unsuccessful attempt to escape me, Chris had moved away from our adjoining bedrooms. When I was still a baby, my father bought the large two-story house in Midtown Memphis for a paltry eighteen grand. It was falling apart, abandoned for so long that stray dogs had grown accustomed to sleeping there, but by the time I'd entered elementary school, my father had remodeled all but a few rooms, one of which was where my brother had chosen to live. Plywood covered one broken window. The walls had holes that exposed wood studs. I walked in without knocking. Years of not being separated by a door had left me unprepared for Chris's sudden need for privacy. He had taken the plywood off the glassless window frame and sat on the outside sill smoking. He startled when I came in, tossed his cigarette into the backyard, and turned around.

"Why don't you knock?"

Without asking, I sat on the floor next to a half-assembled model car, a Chevy Bel Air. Instead of painting it cab yellow, as the instructions suggested, he'd painted it flat black. On a piece of cardboard, he'd practiced drawing flames with a paintbrush. Chris didn't move from the window or ask me to leave. He had on the same purple Rude Dog shirt he wore every day, stonewashed jeans, and Converse shoes. I picked up a small engine and looked it over.

"Put it down," he said. "Glue's still wet."

"Where is everybody?" I asked. "Why's Nana here?"

Chris snorted, shook his head in disgust. He pressed play on the tape deck and Slayer blared from tinny speakers. Chris had changed. The model cars were still the same, but listening to Slayer was new. He got into metal that year when he began seventh grade. The Poison *Flesh and Blood* cassette I bought him for his thirteenth birthday sat unopened next to a pile of car magazines with glossy covers of girls in bikinis.

"You haven't listened to it," I said. "Thought you liked Poison."

"No," he said. "You like Poison."

"Not true, you like them just as much," I said. "You recorded their videos."

We had piles of VHS tapes filled with music videos. After our parents went to bed, we hovered over the record button and waited for the first image or note of our favorite songs. That year, it was "18 and Life" by Skid Row or "Unskinny Bop."

"Poison's pussy metal," Chris said.

"Come on! They're on *Headbanger's Ball*," I said. "Riki Rachtman plays Poison."

"And Riki Rachtman's a pussy," he said.

Whenever Chris lied, his face turned red and a fat vein grew prominent on his forehead. I threw the cassette and the hard plastic hit just above his eye. He wanted to pummel me, but he never did. He never hit me. I hit him, threw things at him, kicked him all the time, but he would never hit back. At most, he'd hold me down until I stopped flailing.

I ran from his room and climbed into my narrow closet, where I'd built a fort by hanging a sheet over the clothes rod. Underneath a folded quilt in the corner, I hid my notebook where I often wrote stories. I was obsessed with a man, a friend of my mother's father, Papa, whose trachea had been removed and who pressed a wand the size of a marker to his throat when he spoke. His voice sounded as if he were talking through a fan. I carried him through my nine-year-old knowledge of the world. I even killed him once—let a drunken bus driver run him down as he crossed Union from the restaurant. I did not write this afternoon but simply sat in the dark until Chris sought me out.

"Don't you hate it? Jimmy's dead, and we're not even allowed to go to the funeral."

It was the first time I'd heard the word *dead* in reference to someone I knew. Opening the door just a little, I said, "You don't know shit."

He nodded, tears already forming. "Uh-huh," he said. "Heard Dad tell Mom." When I put my hand on his shoulder, he knocked it away. "You remember when Jimmy took us on the back porch to watch for tornadoes?" Chris asked. "He was just messing around, but then we saw the funnel over the rooftops. Right then, the sirens started."

"Kind of," I said. I could only picture the shattered truck window.

Chris had nearly four years on me, and his memories included Jimmy more than my own. Jimmy existed in my mind as a collection of sensations—his smell, what I would later learn to be a mixture of cheap beer and sweat; the touch of his wide, taut stomach against my small child chest when hugging him; the sound of Jimmy's loud and breathy laugh that I always recalled simultaneously with my father's low and observant one. Some years before, Papa had bought a cheap freezer and gave it to my family. It worked fine, large and deep, but it was covered with wallpaper featuring fully nude women in high heels and in various erotic poses—some looking inquisitively over the shoulder, some crawling on all fours. My father and Jimmy found Chris and me standing still and stupid and spying on the women as if they might move in their tiny cages. My father barked for us to back off, and Jimmy—young and childless—kissed the snapshots one and one and one. I recall his shiny bald spot and bushy black hair above his ears as he knelt beside the freezer. Busy as both parents were, it took my mother weeks to strip the wallpaper away.

I told Chris about the small bag our father handed off to Deborah.

"Coke," he said.

"It wasn't liquid," I said.

"No," he laughed. "It's a drug."

"What's it do?"

"Makes you hyper."

When our parents came home from the cemetery, Chris and I were playing *Super Mario Brothers 3*. Our father wore black slacks and a blue button-up.

"Get your bags together," he said. "We're going to the river."

When he spoke, his mouth didn't open. It was already late, and the river was a two-hour drive east of Memphis. We owned half an acre on a small wooded property in Birdsong near a nature reserve and a lumber forest of white pine. The Tennessee River, where we swam and fishing boats docked, was close by. I packed my Swiss Army knife, two small lengths of rope, one flashlight, and a change of clothes. I put my ID, quarter for a phone call, and personal-information card into a plastic baggy because we were going near water. All of this was Wolf-badge stuff, easy. Downstairs, our parents fought. "It's not about them," my mother said. "Well damn it! I'm making it about them," my father said.

I found Chris smoking by the broken window. He didn't look confident doing it yet. Our father could build things—use a hammer or work on an engine—while he smoked. Chris looked as if he needed both hands.

"D'ya pack?" I asked.

"Don't need to," he said. "We're coming back tomorrow."

"What about swimming?" I said.

"Why don't you ever knock?" he said.

I slammed his door and kicked it two, three times before I stormed off to my closet. This was our new way. One minute everything was normal, playing and talking, and then he'd need to be alone.

Sometime later, my father opened the door. I felt stupid sitting in the dark and stood to leave. "Wait," he said and put his hands on my shoulders. "I didn't mean to take you to Jimmy's."

That night was special; I had felt as though he needed me. "It's okay," I said.

"Jimmy did something very stupid. Ain't right to take your life. Understand?"

I nodded and followed him out into the hall, where we found Chris sitting on the edge of the top step. He didn't have a bag, just a big felt hat Dad had given him.

"Ready?"

Chris said yes.

"Move your ass, then." Dad pinched Chris's underarms until they both giggled.

By the time we arrived at the river, it was dark. I had fallen asleep and woke up hungry. My father had not changed from his funeral clothes. When we passed by the road toward our piece of land, I whined, "Missed the turn."

"We're making a stop first," my father said.

He turned down a gravel service road where a clean creek flowed. We often loaded up empty milk jugs with water for cooking and drinking. I'd never been down the road at night. The truck heaved over fallen branches and dipped down into potholes. There were signs with the word OPEN written under pictures of deer. Bags of blood hung from branches—"To keep the mosquitoes busy," my father said.

We finally stopped after crossing the creek. Dad cut the headlights but left the motor running. Chris asked, "Why are we here?" He had just woken up too.

"To get water," I said.

"We have water."

Our father got out of the truck, and I watched as he dug out a hatchet and shovel from the bed. Coming around to the passenger side, he opened the glove box and pulled out a cigar box with Jimmy's remains. "Stay in the truck until I come back."

He waded slowly through the roadside brush and disappeared into the dark tree line. Chris rifled out a cigarette from a pack left on the dashboard. I rolled down the windows and cut the ignition. Cold air rushed in from outside. Our father's footsteps echoed through the silent woods. They sounded huge and destructive in all that dark and quiet.

A brief silence followed, and then the first strike of shovel hit ground. A clean *swoosh*, followed by a *thunk*. *Swoosh, thunk.* Chris and I listened, careful not to move. The woods waited too, silent, detecting predator or prey, until my father stopped for so long that the insects began to make noise again. I took out two lengths of rope and practiced a new knot, a bowline—one I didn't need to know yet but had learned anyway. Taking the top loose rope in my left hand and the rest in my right, I pulled, making a loop, and tightened the hitch. A bowline fastens to a post. Under load, it doesn't slip or bind.

I stuck my hand through the open end of the bowline knot and pulled until it was tight against my wrist. The loose ends dangled among my fingers. I leaned out the driver's side window and waited for my father to emerge from the woods. He smiled, but it was a weak smile.

"I want to show you how to find Jimmy," he said. Chris and I met him by the bed of the truck. "There's the creek," he said. "Behind us." He pointed to a small clearing across the road. "That's your second marker." My father told us that he and Jimmy had gone camping out there once and found the meadow. They set up tents and spent the weekend. "Everything's in walking distance," he said. "Creek up on the road, and the river just on the other side of the trees. Drinking water and fishing."

He handed Chris his flashlight. I remembered mine and pulled it out of my bag. With our father in the lead, it seemed as if we walked forever. I tripped over brush, and spiderwebs wrapped around my face. Then I spotted the mound of fresh, wet earth. The name JIMMY cut into the tree bark. No date, no last name. Just Jimmy. My father stood with his arm resting on the tree, eyes closed. I shined my light around, looking for Chris, and found him standing a few feet behind me.

"Shut your lights," my father said. "I'm here."

Reluctantly, I cut mine off and stood in the dark waiting for my eyes to adjust to the new, paler light of the moon. The woods deepened with sounds unknown to us, with hidden movement, until our eyes focused on the freshly turned earth and the carving in the tree.

III   Here

My brother called out that someone was living in the forest. I ran
to his voice and came upon a camp: one mattress with blankets,
a cooler, and a small battery-powered radio. When Chris told me
to open the cooler, I did as he said. I stepped across the mattress,
squatted, and opened the cooler so slowly that every muscle in my
body twitched. Inside, dirty water sloshed around a single can of
beer and a plastic bag with bread and cheese so flowered with mold
that together those sandwich goods looked extraterrestrial. I shot
past Chris and back into the open lane, where I found my father,
shirtless, cowboy hat tilted back—"What y'all get into now?" We
were shy when we answered, but it seemed as though he wanted
us to *get into* something, as though he wanted us to dig up trouble.
He brought my brother and me to the Arkansas floodplain so that
we might play in the woods, as he once had as a child. After all, it
was our Sunday together. Or rather, it was his.

On our way out, later that day, Dad drove down dirt roads for
miles, changing out one rutted lane for another until we were
finally alongside the Mississippi River. Chris and I rode on the

bumper, my guts rattling as we passed over potholes. I imagined myself as an action hero, and I grabbed hold of the trailer hitch of a fleeing villain's ride and dropped down, my stomach hitting the ground with a hard *thunk*. I can still recall how scared I felt when my shoes were yanked out from beneath me. I held on. Dust from the road gathered around my face, and rocks dug into my denim jacket, tearing a hole in the thigh of my jeans. Chris yelled STOP, but my father had the radio up loud as he sang along with "Hotel California," his voice pleasantly harmonizing—I remember that, thinking he sounded nice, wishing I could sing like him—as the ground jutted and popped beneath me. A pebble hit my temple, just barely missing my eye, and I let go.

At first the momentum continued to pull me forward even though my body wasn't attached to anything. I rolled over and over on the hard gravel. When I finally stopped and stood, the truck was much farther up the road than I had anticipated. I could see the silhouette of Dad's cowboy hat, his elbow stuck out of the driver's side window. Chris had hitched his leg over the tailgate, calling for him to stop. They drove over a rise, and for a moment, I lost sight of them. It all happened within a matter of seconds, and before they returned, before my brother took a turn dragging behind the truck, and before my father let Chris drive so that he, too, could enjoy the fun, I stood there, bruised, with most of the buttons torn off my jacket, angry with myself for acting rashly and intensely aware of being alone with no recognizable markers to lead me back home.

IV   The Junk Trade

Junk Man Wayne was set to meet my father at seven. Even though my watch alarm beeped on the hour, I still checked the time every few minutes. I sat cross-legged on the floor next to Chris, watching sitcoms in the dimly lit front room. My father had just come home from his construction job. He'd bathed and put on a pair of clean clothes before joining us. Eyes red with fatigue, he leaned forward in his recliner and smoked.

Mom curled up on the end of the couch closest to my father. Her four-foot-ten and ninety-pound frame barely covered half the cushion. "I was about to load this old vanity, when a red-and-white truck pulled up and Wayne stepped out," she told my father. "Weren't no need for me to bring that dresser home, and so I let him take it, seeing it's how he makes a living. If I ran a junk business, I'd never let nothin' go."

My mother often drove around upscale neighborhoods, scouting out heaps of furniture, clothes, toys, and dishes. Sometimes she'd leave right after dinner or run an hour late picking me up from school because she'd happened by a particularly handsome pile.

"Sidewalk shopping," she called it. She'd recognized Wayne as the stepfather of Chris's friend Kevin. He told her he needed help at the flea market, and she volunteered her sons.

My father didn't like the idea of me working for anyone besides him. Often, he paid Chris and me three dollars an hour to clean up after a job finished or before a remodel began. Wayne offered fifteen bucks for three hours of work.

"Won't be like when you work with me," my father said. "No talk back. No *I'm tired.*"

"I won't ask you for money," I said. I'd just started going steady with a girl named Tatum and daydreamed about taking her out on a date, buying her a watch like mine.

My alarm beeped. I'd thrown away the instruction manual and had no idea how to set it. I could only make the sound stop by pressing all four buttons. It was an adult watch, too big for my bone-thin wrist. But it glowed in the dark, and I could hold it underwater when bathing.

When Wayne knocked on the door, Chris stood up and took his plate into the kitchen. Mom told me to wait. The junk man's flannel shirt stretched over his large belly, and a hedge of bushy hair stuck out below a camouflage ball cap. He shook my hand and told Dad I didn't look big enough to carry my own pecker.

"Unloaded that vanity yet?" Mom asked.

"About come to blows with your wife over that dresser," Wayne said to Dad, and both men laughed. Mom smiled, but she wrung her hands. Most nooks and shelves in our house were covered in her found kitsch: decorative tin cans with snowmen riding sleds, glass bottles in dark greens and browns, an antique porcelain doll with a giant hole taken out of one cheek. Collecting furniture was her current love.

"Make yourself scarce," Dad told me. "Let us grown-ups talk."

I found Chris in the backyard tossing a ball to our dog. Mom had originally wanted Chris to take the job, but he wasn't interested. He'd just turned fourteen and rarely left his room. When I asked

Chris why he didn't want the job, he told me he'd already worked for Wayne before, back when he still hung out with Kevin.

"Why didn't you say so?" I asked.

Chris shrugged and looked away. He mumbled something about Wayne being an asshole. The dog panted. "Go bug someone else," Chris said.

Wayne had already left when I came back inside, but the deal was done. He'd pick me up for work at six o'clock the next morning. My father said, "You do everything he tells you." And my mother asked if I knew the way home in case I got sick; the fairgrounds, where Wayne set up his stall, were five blocks from the house. Dad shut her down. "You don't leave early, even if you are sick," he said. "Tough it out."

I called Tatum. The downstairs phone had a sixty-foot cord. From the front room, I could carry the receiver all the way to the back porch. My favorite nook was the small playroom with a Nintendo and cable hooked up to a black-and-white television. I shut the cord in the door. Besides the night we met at a sleepover my friend Max orchestrated when his parents went out of town, Tatum and I hadn't spent any time together. We didn't share classes or recess because she was in sixth grade while I was in fifth. She was also thirteen to my ten and technically should have been in junior high, but she had been held back. For the most part, we spent time on the phone, barely saying a word, watching television together. I told her about the job. "Thought I could take you to a movie when I get paid."

She held her hand over the mouthpiece and said, "He's got a job," to someone else.

"Who you talking to?"

"My mom."

I could hear music in the background. "I'm on MTV," she said. I changed the channel to match hers.

During the sleepover at Max's—after we'd watched television and played tag, Hail Mary, and charades—Tatum suggested playing truth or dare. According to her, the game involved spinning a wine bottle, but we made due with an empty two liter of Orange Crush. At first the truths and dares were innocent enough: Max kissed the toilet seat, Tatum drank a concoction of condiments. But quickly each turn grew more sexual: Liz dared Max to kiss me on the mouth; Max dared Liz to kiss Tatum; Tatum dared Liz to show her breasts; Liz dared Tatum and me to spend seven minutes in heaven. Tatum took my hand and led me into Max's room. "Come on," she said, "Let's get this over with." I closed Max's door and turned on the lights. Tatum gave me a sheepish look and turned them off again. She took my hands and led me to Max's bed. I'd never kissed before, but I'd seen how actors did in movies. Each twist of my tongue against hers reminded me of the rubber wrestlers Chris and I used to play with, Hulk Hogans and Pretty Boy Floyds with slots opened in the back that we jammed our thumbs through. Making out with Tatum was the first time I'd explored a body that was not my own, and my nerves were equally repelled and attracted by the softness of her skin.

When Wayne and I arrived at the fairgrounds, we drove to the far corner of a massive parking lot where a few vendors had already begun setting up stalls. The sun hadn't made it over the low-slung buildings yet. Everything was cast in a gray, early November light. Though I wore my flannel shirt and a jean jacket, I was still very cold.

Wayne pulled out a folding table. "Set this up," he said.

I laid the table flat on the ground but couldn't get the legs to expand. Frustrated and embarrassed that something so simple had bested me, I yelled, "Damn thing!" Wayne saw me struggling and came over. "Give me your hand." Holding my small palm against a lever, he said, "Squeeze," and the leg unhitched from the lock.

I unpacked plastic tubs and set up an eclectic array of rusted light fixtures, clocks, toys and dolls, board games, and VHS tapes on the foldout tables. Inside one bin labeled Valuables were four glass jewelry cases that held watches, belt buckles, perfume bottles, earrings, and necklaces. I noticed a pocket watch with a military insignia—earth speared by an anchor and in the clutches of an eagle. I'd never seen a watch like that before. I checked the tag—twenty-five dollars—and buried it at the bottom of the case, hoping no one would buy it before I could.

"Help me drag out your mama's vanity," Wayne said.

Climbing into the back of the truck, I pushed the dresser up to the tailgate, stepped down. I held the legs as tight as I could, but the dresser was too heavy for me to carry. To keep from dropping my end, I leaned back against the tailgate. Green paint chipped away. Underneath the paint was a dark stain with thick splits in the wood.

"Thought you were grown enough for the job?" Wayne winked. "Listen, I'm gonna put my end down. Slow as I can. You just stay there. Don't move."

He shimmied behind me and took hold of the legs. I could feel the soft of his stomach press against my back. "I'll lift up and give you some room to crawl out," he said. The angle forced me to slide so close to his body that I could smell the sour sweat of his jeans.

Tatum and I went to the movies the following weekend. My mom was hesitant about letting us go out alone but relented when Tatum's mom agreed to meet with her. On a Friday night, my mother drove me to Highland Park Cinema, and she and I waited in her minivan for the little red convertible.

Mom had the radio tuned to the oldies station; she sang along to "Brown Eyed Girl," bouncing in her seat and waving her arms over to me. "Car dance," she said. "Come on, honey, car dance." But Tatum was half an hour late, and I didn't feel like car dancing. "Used to love the car dance," Mom said, glowering. She lit a cigarette, inhaled, and looked out across the parking lot. Boxes full of papers, manila envelopes, and photo albums filled the back seat. I asked her why she wanted some stranger's old pictures and journals. "They're memories, honey," she said. "You can't throw out memories."

Around a quarter to six, Tatum's mom pulled up in front of the theater. The red convertible squealed off before I was out of the van. "So much for meet-the-parents," Mom said.

At the theater entrance, Tatum hugged my waist, leaning her head on my shoulder. "My mom's having a tantrum," she said. "She thinks her boyfriend's cheating on her."

I didn't know how to respond. Once, Mom got overcharged at Ike's Grocery, and back home, staring down at the receipt, she yelled, "That fucker cheated me out of thirty cents."

I rubbed Tatum's back like boys in movies did when girls were upset. "You're sweet," Tatum said and kissed me on the mouth at the very moment Mom pulled up next to us and honked her horn. We jolted apart.

"I'll be back by eight," Mom said.

Inside the auditorium, I asked Tatum, "What row?"

She pointed to the front, and I followed with our large popcorn and drink. I held her hand and leaned over to ask if she was all right. She kissed me, and as we kissed, separated by plastic armrests and our giant Coke, I had no idea what to do with my hands. I held one under my thigh, while the other clutched her seat. She loosened my grip and pulled my hand toward her knee, and I knocked our drink to the floor. I jerked away, frantically trying to figure out a way to stop the stream of Coke and ice that was spreading beneath us.

"Forget it," Tatum said.

I laid my hand against her waist, and she untucked her shirt. My alarm beeped the hour as Tatum guided my hand against the firm padding of her bra. The watch face glowed neon through her pink shirt. I clasped all four buttons until the beeping stopped.

The next morning, my father made coffee in the kitchen as I waited for Wayne. He smoked with his arms resting on his knees and his hair hung loose over his face. This was the first time we'd been alone together in months. I sat still and alert to his every move. The coffeepot gurgled and spat, and he stood to pour a cup, wearing only a red union suit with the back flap half-unbuttoned. Midstride, he paused and clamped his abdomen. The way his body tensed as the pain took him surprised me, and I asked if he were okay. I had no way of understanding sustained bodily damage or illness. That morning, he simply seemed old.

A photo hung in the dining room just beyond the table where we sat—my father, in tight white jeans with no shirt, sitting astride a Harley Chopper, with my older sister, Kim, perched happily in front of him. I often stared at this photo and dreamed of the day I, too, would ride a motorcycle through town shirtless in tight white pants.

My father surprised me when he pushed a full cup of coffee across the table and said, "Have some?" I coughed as it went down hot in the back of my throat. It was bitter.

"Too strong?" My father laughed. "Put hair on your chest, that's for sure."

He always said that whenever I didn't like something adults did. I added two more spoons of sugar and a lot more milk. What I got tasted like dirty ice cream, but I wanted my father to believe I liked it. When Wayne pulled up, he said, "Don't work too hard. It'll keep you young."

A steady wind made getting the stall set up unbearable. Wayne stayed in the truck while I laid out the tub marked Valuables. I dug around the case until I found the military watch. The spring had come unwound, as it did every week. While I set the analog time to my digital, Wayne called me over, suggesting we wait in the heated cab until a customer drifted by.

Once I climbed inside, he cranked the heat. Trash was piled up on the floorboard around my feet, and a box of snack cakes and chips sat in the space between us. Underneath the smell of coffee, cigarette smoke, and body odor, something warm, homey, lurked inside Wayne's truck. He tapped a cigarette from his pack and lit up, blowing a thick cloud of smoke through his clenched teeth.

"What you like to do?" Wayne asked.

"Nothing, really," I said. His question shook me, and suddenly I could not think of a single thing worth sharing with an adult. I liked MTV. I liked Pearl Jam and Nirvana. I'd recently read Bradbury's *Martian Chronicles*. Dad didn't like those things, so why would Wayne care?

"You got a girlfriend?"

"Yeah," I said. I told him about making out at the movies, and he listened.

"Woo-wee," he said, sucking air through his teeth. "Watch out for them feisty ones."

Wayne pulled another cigarette from his pack and lit it off the old, sparks popping from the cherry. Only one side lit, and Wayne said, "Means somebody's thinking about my dick." He caught my eye, a sheepish look on his face. "You want one?"

I took the cigarette.

"How long you smoked?"

"A year," I lied. It was my first time.

"I started around ten, too."

And I liked that Wayne didn't say I was too young. I leaned back in my seat with the lit cigarette between my fingers. I drew smoke into my mouth and held it between my cheeks, warm against my teeth, before blowing out a thick cloud.

"Hey now." He motioned with his hand for me to move away from the window. "Can't have anybody seeing you smoke."

Wayne moved his box of food onto the dash, opening up a space in the seat between us. "Watch me," he said. He cupped the cigarette into the palm of his hand, and it disappeared. "No one sees, right?" Wayne took a drag from the hidden cigarette and bent down close to my lap, blowing the smoke toward the floorboard.

"Now you," he said.

I held the cigarette like he had shown me and took a drag. When I bent down, Wayne put his hand on my neck and guided me closer to his lap. I stiffened. My parents always told us kids that we should never let a grown up touch us. Just the year before, we watched a three-hour-long documentary about abducted, murdered children. But strangers took those kids, and Wayne had been invited to the house.

"Stay down low," he said, lifting his hand from my neck.

All I could see was the gas pedal and the crotch of his jeans. I rose back up and stared out the window for a while. Playing it cool, I kept the cigarette hidden in my hand. Taking another drag, I bent down toward his side of the truck again, but this time I leaned closer to the car radio. Again, he guided my head between his legs. "Don't tell nobody," he said. "Anyone finds out, and we'll both be in deep shit."

Tatum and I hid in the round plastic bubble of our elementary school play tower long after school had let out. Normally, she'd walk home, but I'd convinced my mom to pick me up late so we could spend time together. The globe cast an orange light on us as we kissed.

According to my watch, Mom was running twenty minutes late.

"I'm gonna walk home," Tatum said.

I waited for a long time after she left, standing at the top of the tower, wanting to slide but fearing I would look dumb. When Mom finally honked, I'd gotten over being angry and had started to worry.

"Where's Tatum?"

"Home," I said. "She couldn't wait any longer."

Mom apologized for being late. "Thought you two wanted more time together."

A narrow, long-backed chair sat cramped on the back seat. I saw boxes of what looked like toys. "What'd you find this time?" I asked.

"Oh, you'll love it," she said. "There's He-Men and some of those little blue guys that look like Smurfs but aren't. Some dolls."

She drove in the opposite direction of home, and when I asked her where we were going, she said, "Back by that house."

"I'm starving."

Fifteen minutes later, we pulled to a stop in front of a house in an upscale neighborhood.

"Need your help with the boxes," she said.

The thought of people watching Mom scavenge was what I hated the most. She stepped out; her legs, the muscles ravaged by polio, were gaunt under beige capris pants. The left knee buckled as she stepped onto the curb. There were about fifteen boxes on the sidewalk. I rolled down the window, and cold air rushed in. "All the boxes?"

"Just the toys," she said, showing me the GI Joe snowmobile I once coveted.

"I don't want to, Mom."

"Oh, so it's cool when Wayne does it, but not me?" she said.

I threw open the sliding van door. As I wrangled some other kid's toys into the back, Mom opened a box and dug through it on the spot.

"What are you gonna do with all this?" I asked. "We don't play with toys anymore."

She slapped the box closed and began walking toward the driver's side. "It's nice stuff," she said. "I never had stuff this nice."

Because Wayne was interested, I told him stories, like how Tatum and I had snuck into a storage room at the Oak Court Mall. Christmas decorations had recently been stowed away, and a giant Santa head stuck out from piles of fake snow. But his questions always pointed toward sex—"You touch her coochie?" And because I wanted to impress him, I lied—"We totally kiss naked all the time."

I decided I would quit working for Wayne. When I told Mom that I wanted to quit, she only said, "Your daddy's been telling everybody about how you're holding down a job."

I waited on the porch for Dad to get home from work. "What's the word, thunderbird?" he said as he stepped from his truck.

"Got to talk to you about something."

His back straightened. He held his lunch pail in one hand

and a squished pack of cigarettes in the other. Paint and sawdust covered his denim jacket and jeans. When I told him I wanted to quit working for Wayne, he let out a breath.

I'd drawn together a nest of excuses that were all true: Wayne didn't pay me what he said he would, Wayne made me smoke between his legs, Wayne talked dirty. Instead, I blurted out, "I stand outside all day in the cold while he sits in the truck with the heat on."

Dad smiled and lit a cigarette. I could see my reflection in his aviators. My eyes were too big for my thin face, too eager. "First job I had, I was maybe twelve, I dug a foundation for a house. Eight hours in the scorching heat. When I went to get paid, the fat bastard told me I'd have to wait till next week. Never saw that money." Dad laughed to himself. "Got to take a lot of grief before you can sit up in the heated truck. Just how the world works. Stick it out one more week, and you'll be fine."

When I met Tatum's mother face-to-face, we drove to Shelby Forest on a Sunday with the intention of riding horses. I'd never been around a horse and was terrified. Tatum's grandparents had taken her riding the summer before, and she told me about how her horse had jerked the reins from her mother's grip and bolted up the trail away from the adults. "I've never been happier than on that horse," she said.

Tatum's mom and her mom's boyfriend, Dan, left us at the car while they went to fetch the horses. Fifteen minutes later, the two adults rode up on large brown beasts with blonde manes. I waited for mine to come trotting down the trail, but no others followed. "Y'all behave now," her mom said. "We'll be back in an hour."

Tatum and I had been going steady for five months at that point, and it was the first time I'd seen her cry. She locked herself in the car. I busied myself climbing a tree until the adults returned.

Later that afternoon, Tatum's mom rented *Dances with Wolves* and bought pizza. The four of us set up camp in front of the television—Tatum and I on the floor, the adults on the couch.

Twenty minutes into the movie, her mom said, "Tatum, honey, I'm gonna take a nap. Make sure you get me up in time to take him home." She and Dan walked to the far end of the hall. I heard the door to her mom's room lock.

"Come here," Tatum said without turning around.

I lay down behind her and put my arms around her waist. "Mom's so stupid," she said. I rubbed her back, but when I rose up to kiss her, she said, "Don't," and brought my arm between her legs. My wristwatch caught on her dress and pulled a thread loose.

"God," she said. "Take this stupid watch off."

She guided my arm under the hem and moved my wristbone between her legs. I leaned over to kiss her, and again she said, "Don't." Her legs tightened over my arm. The noises she made under her breath sounded eerily adult. I wouldn't discover masturbation for another year, but at thirteen, Tatum was an older woman. And as she rubbed herself against my arm, I grew bored, resting my head on my free hand, watching Kevin Costner ride a horse through an open meadow. When she made an *ouch* noise, I thought I'd hurt her.

"What happened?"

"Thank you," she said. "I needed that."

The last day I worked for Wayne, he sold Mom's vanity. Though it was cold and Wayne bugged me to sit with him inside the truck, I hung around outside by the tables. Wearing gloves and a knit hat, I talked up a pearl-handled shaving knife to a man with yellow tobacco stains in his beard. An elderly woman bought a rusted-shut coal lantern. I wiped the glass cases with Windex and alternated between winding the military watch and hiding it when a customer sauntered by.

Just after it started to snow, a woman appeared and asked, "How much that dresser going for?" She wore a Tweety Bird T-shirt with lace fringe around the neckline. I told her Wayne wanted $150.

"Hey," she called to the truck, ignoring me. "Hey! This boy thinks trash is gold."

Wayne stepped out of the truck, asking her how much she was willing to pay. The exchange went quickly. The woman said fifty, and Wayne told her seventy-five plus delivery. I thought about my mom. Wayne cared about the money, but Mom cared about something entirely different. Though I had no way of articulating it then, I can see now that what she wanted was the memento. The object itself intrigued her—*Can't throw out memories.* The snow thickened after the woman left, and I had no choice but to climb into Wayne's truck. My fingers were numb. Wayne handed me a cup of coffee. Unlike the sweet and milky stuff I'd started drinking with Dad on those early Saturday mornings before we both went off to work, the coffee Wayne handed me was black. It burned my tongue, and I spit it back into the cup.

Wayne patted my back. "There you go," he said, rubbing his fingers along my shoulder. "Tell me more about this little lady you got."

"Nothing to say," I said. Each time I thought about lying on the floor in Tatum's living room, an uneasy feeling rose in my gut.

Wayne took a drink of coffee, and after setting his Styrofoam cup back into the console, he rested his hand on my thigh. With both of my hands wrapped around the cup for warmth, I stared into the steam, watching the vapor thin. He ran his finger down the inside of my leg. Slow. "Does she touch you like this?" His touch was gentle. My nerves stood on end the way they had that first night I kissed Tatum. When I didn't respond, he moved his finger up my thigh, closer to my crotch, and I felt trapped beneath the light, soft weight of his hand.

"Like this?" He cupped his fingers around my dick. The moist warmth of his grip heated the deep recesses of my groin. Wayne's fingers stroked my balls, and they twitched and shrunk.

I opened the truck door. "I'm gonna look around," I said. Wayne's hand jerked away. Out in the falling snow, I waited for his permission to leave. He tapped the steering wheel, staring straight ahead.

"Hold on," he said, and he handed me a twenty-dollar bill. "Pick up some doughnuts while you're at it," he said. "Keep the change."

Most outdoor vendors had packed up, but a stubborn few strung tarpaulins over their booths and stared out into the white. I did not intend to buy anything, but I pretended to look at chain saws and drills; jewelry and purses; clothes and shoes. Browsing gave me something to do while I calmed. I couldn't shake Wayne's touch. I could've walked home. I envisioned Dad driving me back and the two of us kicking Wayne's ass. But I felt indebted to Wayne, a little greedy besides. After all, if I stayed on, I'd take in my regular pay on top of whatever was left after buying doughnuts. Eventually I ventured indoors. The place was packed with people taking shelter from the snow, and I pushed through the crowd until I reached the stand. I bought a chocolate doughnut with sprinkles, Wayne's favorite, and a jelly filled for myself.

At the stall, I ate my doughnut in the snow, and he didn't stop me. But now that it was done, now that I had my doughnut and an extra eighteen dollars, I was angry with Wayne. I didn't know any other way to express my complete powerlessness besides stealing the military watch. I took it out of the case, with its long chain and world-clutching eagle, and slipped it into my coat pocket. It was the first thing I'd ever stolen, and I immediately feared reprisal. But instead of putting it back, I unclasped my own wristwatch and shoved it in among the junk.

The following summer, the five o'clock news dedicated a segment to Wayne. His stepchildren had come forward as victims. Beyond having a restraining order issued, Wayne's punishment was to keep a large yellow sign in his front yard, alerting neighbors that he was a convicted sex offender. When my parents saw the report, I was not downstairs but in Chris's bedroom watching MTV. My father screamed for us. We stared at one another, uncertain of the crime we were being summoned to answer for, and he yelled a second time, emphasizing that he would not yell a third. We rushed to our punishment.

"Did he touch you," my father screamed. He was pointing to the television. "Speak up, goddamn it! Did he touch you? Either of you?" I immediately recognized Wayne's house.

I looked to Chris for answers. Until that moment, I'd never considered that Wayne might also have touched him. He shook his head. My father's face lightened.

"No," I said.

When we were back upstairs, I told Chris the truth. He was sitting on the bed, a metal serving tray with rolling papers and tobacco on his lap. He rolled a cigarette, and I asked if I could have one too. He said I was too young.

"Fuck you. I smoke already."

"Yeah, when?"

"With Wayne."

Chris handed me the cigarette. "You know why I stopped working? It was because—" I could still feel Wayne's hand each time I thought about his truck, ashamed I couldn't separate the sensuality of his touch from Tatum's. Chris watched me and waited. "Did he touch you too?" I asked. He shook his head, but I'd later learn this was a lie.

My face was red, blotchy in the mirror. I pulled smoke into my cheeks. Chris laughed at me. He held his cigarette comically high and took a drag. "That's what you look like," he said. "You're not smoking if you don't breathe it into your lungs. Otherwise, you're just faking."

I inhaled deeply and was surprised when I began to choke, coughing until my stomach hurt. But I did not want to fake it, and so when the fit cleared, I inhaled a second time.

V   Superman Dam Fool

1.

My mother and I drove downtown so that I could reenroll in junior high after an arrest and suspension. It was a humid Memphis spring, and two men leaned against the sidewall of a liquor store, sharing a bottle wrapped in brown paper. The words SUPERMAN DAM FOOL covered the length of brickwork in white paint, each letter composed uncertainly, as if by a different hand. Drawn next to the words was a stick figure—a smiling circle and a legless, armless bar. It wore no cape. DC Comics had just killed Superman. Every comic seller in the city sold his demise. Rows of bloodied Ss filled the racks.

I have no idea how long the graffiti had been up or if it was in response to the death of Superman, but at the time, I wondered. In fact, I wonder still. For what reason was Superman foolish?

2.

In third grade I told Ashley Pettigrew that I knew how to cuss without getting in trouble. "Dam it," I said. My feet barely scraped the dirt as I hung from the monkey bars. "That is spelled d-a-m-n," Ashley told me. "Dam is spelled d-a-m. So you're not really cussing."

3.

The thing about aging is that I now welcome tallying my failure and humiliation. It elicits the same pleasure as cleaning house after a busy month or painting a room instead of bleaching out scuff marks. But it's the ambiguity within morality, the difference between guilt and innocence that eludes me. I have a working knowledge of foolishness.

4.

The Superman issues that led to his death each ended with a bleak panel of a creature sheathed in what looks like a hazmat suit banging chained paws against a steel container buried deep in the earth: DOOMSDAY IS COMING! Once freed, popping up somewhere in the Midwest, Doomsday extended his hand for a yellow canary to land. He crushed the bird. The caption BLORCH hovered next to his fist in bloodred letters—"HAH . . . HA HA HAAA."

5.

Did the graffiti artist believe Superman was a fool because he used his powers to fight evil instead of, say, vacationing in the Bahamas? It is true that Superman would never have had to wait in transportation lines, and if he wanted, he could have easily won Mr. Universe pageants or literally picked up any woman, or man, he desired. What's the use of morality when you are a superior being?

6.

In kindergarten I sold my soul to the devil. I'd been punished, sent out into the hall, for using my hand to make fart sounds under my arm during nap time. Right when giggles subsided, I'd let another one rip, only to bring on a fresh bout of laughter. I'd never been so popular. According to my older brother, Chris, the devil granted wishes. I can't remember what I wished for, but a desire to be beyond punishment lingers in my memory.

7.

Chris knew all about the devil, because at ten years old he was a Satanist. He'd been converted, he said, when he found *The Satanic Bible* glowing on a corner shelf in his elementary school library. I was plump with wishes, but when I told Chris that I'd asked the devil to kidnap our little sister, Amanda, after she'd left my Big Wheel out front and it was stolen, he said, "Take it back. Satan's evil."

8.

On the day of my arrest and suspension from junior high, I'd just come back from a six-week-long sick leave—pneumonia, mono, glandular infection—when the vice principal found a razor blade in my wallet. The real principal had just been arrested for embezzlement, and the vice principal had been temporarily promoted. Finals neared, and to make up for the time I lost while sick, I'd obtained a hall pass to study in the library instead of attending English. Along the way, I ran into a kid I knew who sold his Ritalin prescription during lunchtime, and after that, the two of us ran into the interim principal. My friend didn't have a hall pass, and our persons were searched for drugs or weapons. The interim principal told us he was cracking down on school violence. Two different students had been stabbed with pencils that year alone. During his tenure, each morning, the homeroom bell was withheld until the yellow buses unloaded teenagers who lived full-time at the county juvenile penitentiary. At day's end, the buses idled, waiting for the nonincarcerated students to leave campus.

9.

Superman fought Doomsday all across the plains. Furious with primal rage, uttering preverbal caws, grunts, and growls, the subterranean creature matched Superman's prowess. "He wants destruction and death," Superman told Lois Lane while barreling the creature through a brick wall with his powerful heat vision. "I have to be every bit as ferocious and unrelenting as he is."

To which Lois, dressed in a skirt, high heels, and a business blazer with especially geometric shoulder pads, cried, "But . . . you can't."

10.

I spent the first year of my life with steel between my legs. A rod held my feet apart and bound my ankles. "Realignment," the doctor told my mother. My leg joints and hip sockets were incompatible. Later, I wore braces with hard-plastic-covered springs that held together leather straps and connected to brown corrective shoes.

During recess, when the other boys played soccer, I wandered the outer corridors of the school, the springs of my braces creaking in the cool, smaller alcoves. Children were forbidden to leave the playground, and my kindergarten teacher repeatedly had to search me out. One day, she handed me a rusted coffee can full of water and a brush. "Here," she said. "Color the bricks." With a few strokes, the rust-colored bricks shined crimson and new. I looked up, paintbrush dripping droplets in the dust, just as two boys whose names I've forgotten but whose white sneakers I still recall ran all the way from girls who jumped rope by the front door to the swing set at the far end of the lot.

By summer break, I had become a master brick painter. My favorite things to paint were arrows that ended near bushes or walls, as if I had access to secret corridors the other children would never know. Sometimes I hid across from the water-painted arrows and waited, hoping someone would see that I'd vanished.

11.

Not only could Superman fly, but he also had x-ray vision, superhuman strength, and superhuman speed. And he never aged or suffered any lasting wounds. The Man of Steel. But Clark Kent, the reporter persona that Superman used to closet his identity, was just a normal guy. Not only normal but socially inept, clumsy, and in many ways invisible, especially to Lois Lane.

A month before he was killed, Superman was set to marry Lois

Lane. Superman lived outside the bounds of time. Each conquest, each adventure had no past, nor future. If Superman were to marry Lois, then this would force him into the realm of mortality, ultimately normalizing Superman and killing Clark Kent.

12.

Inside the Velcro pouch of my wallet, the interim principal found a rusted roofing blade. Unlike a normal razor blade, this one hooked inward. My wallet was red with a rainbow and unicorn. I'd found the blade in the woods when my family went camping two summers before. I'd wanted to make a weapon for my favorite GI Joe, Shipwreck. Shipwreck had long since been stored in the attic. The cop who escorted me off campus in handcuffs believed my story. "Used to make weapons for my toys," he said. "Had a stick with a razor blade that my He-Man carried around."

13.

While smashing up a Lex-Mart, Doomsday was distracted by a commercial that advertised wrestling at the Metropolis Arena. A wrestler yelled, "WHERE ARE YOU GONNA GO?" And as if awakened to some greater purpose, Doomsday repeated, "'MHH-TRR-PLSS?'" In the city, Doomsday raged against skyscrapers, shopping plazas, media stations, and Superman. If Kent is Superman's alter ego, then Doomsday is the id that Superman must restrain, rebury deep below the surface. During a fight that takes place early in the issue, Superman literally attempts to muscle the creature back into the earth: "I DON'T KNOW WHAT HOLE YOU CRAWLED OUT OF—BUT I'M SENDING YOU BACK!" In the end, Superman and Doomsday miraculously serve simultaneous blows that leave them both dead in the rubble.

14.

Perhaps I'm misreading the graffiti and DAM literally refers to damming, as one dams a river. If I drove to the liquor store late one night and painted THE between DAM and FOOL and added a comma and an S and exclamation point at the end, it would then read, "SUPERMAN, DAM THE FOOLS!"—a command or a plea.

15.

Once, as a teenager, while having a conversation with a friend about literature, I was told I didn't like Virginia Woolf because I did not try hard enough, to which I replied, "Perhaps you try too hard." Years later, when I *actually* read Woolf for the first time, it was her diaries I loved most.

16.

"I enjoy epicurean ways of society; sipping and then shutting my eyes to taste. I enjoy almost everything," Woolf wrote on February 27, 1926. "Yet I have some restless searcher in me. Why is there not a discovery in life? Something one can lay hands on and say, 'This is it'?"

17.

After selling my soul, my brother and I found a hurt puppy in the road. Because we fought over whose room the puppy would sleep in, my mother set up a box in the hallway. That night, after everyone went to sleep, I snuck out and cuddled the sleeping dog. Sometime later, a ghost—a man in a suit and tie—appeared at the end of the hall and walked toward me. Because I'd rescinded my deal with the devil, I anticipated this arrival, and oddly, I felt relieved.

18.

When my braces were finally removed, the summer between my first and second year of elementary school, I was given a pair of corrective shoes that looked deceptively like basketball sneakers. Back at the house, my mother told me to run. I'd never been able to run. "I'm going around the block," I said. It was strange, running, not like flying at all. My left leg was stiff in the hip socket, and the sneakers felt bulky on my feet. At the corner of my street, I tripped on the toe of my new shoes and scraped my knee on the sidewalk. "Pussy!" my neighbor Zachariah yelled from his porch. I stood, ran faster than I had before, and yelled, "Damn you!"

19.

Superman didn't really die. He came back a year later, in an issue called "Reign of the Superman". He'd changed. Superman was more suspicious than before, guarded.

Doomsday was also revived, and his origin revealed. One of Superman's countrymen, 250,000 years prior, had forced subjects into extremely hostile environments and then cloned the tissue of those that survived. Eventually, Doomsday, a product of this experiment, grew superior and killed everything on the planet, including Superman's ancestor.

20.

While searching my friend's bag, the interim principal stuck his finger on a safety pin holding down a Nirvana patch. It bled a little, and he yelled for the nurse—"God knows! Now I've got to get checked for AIDS."

"I don't have AIDS," the kid said. "Why would I have AIDS?" He began to cry.

21.

Sometimes I imagine that the graffiti artist's Superman refers not to the comic hero but to a friend of the artist. Perhaps Superman the friend liked to get drunk on fortified wine and act a damn fool. Maybe he liked to run down busy streets, naked, and singing, "IwantmybabybackbabybackbabybackbabybackIwantmybabyback-babybackbabybackbaby—"

22.

The year after I was arrested, in the eighth grade, I lied to the interim principal and told him that another boy had pulled a gun on me. I wanted to transfer out. The gun was real, but it had only been threatened—"When you ain't looking," the boy who jumped me in the bathroom had said. I was laid out in the urinal with a bloodied nose. "Pop." He held two fingers together and pressed them against my forehead. I knew him from the year before. When he skipped me in the lunch line, I choked him. Back in the seventh grade, my friends and I had learned that people beat you up less when you acted crazy.

One friend chose to bang his head against the wooden desk until it bled. This worked for a while, but when I was out sick, a group of boys cornered him in the stairwell and ripped out every facial piercing he had: three eyebrow, two nostril, and three lip rings. They even managed to tear his earlobe. He was the first to drop out of school. When I asked him why the others jumped him, he scoffed. "I forget," he said. "Does it matter?"

23.

"The truth is," Woolf wrote in 1926, "one can't write directly about the soul. Looked at, it vanishes; but look at the ceiling, at Grizzle, at the cheaper beasts in the Zoo which are exposed to walkers in Regent's Park, and the soul slips in."

24.

Later in the postresurrection series, Superman relishes beating up villains instead of trying to avoid it. When he is forced to kill a cyborg imposter of himself, he does so by ramming his fist through his robotic doppelganger's stomach, lifting him in the air, and through a simple spasm of arm muscle, he shatters his likeness into a million little pieces.

25.

After watching Ralph Macchio in *The Karate Kid*, I became an expert black belt. Unlike Macchio, I didn't need a Mr. Miyagi, because my fleece karate outfit came with the belt already attached. Chris had one too, but he chose to sleep in his rather than wear it to school. I preferred real-life heroism to superpowers.

26.

A low brick wall ran in serpentine fashion along the front of our elementary school. Once, at the end of the day, I found Chris caught up in a fight. A boy, bigger than Chris, threw pinecones at Chris's face as he lay on the ground, hiding his head with his arms. Neither my brother nor the bully saw me as I stood up on the brick wall. And neither boy saw when I jumped, kicking the bully in the back with both feet. I didn't anticipate the pain that came when I landed on my hip, and I tried hard not to whimper. The bully lay in front of me, screaming, running his fingers all along his spine as if he meant to fling away fire ants. Chris raised his head from the ground and saw the bully, and then he saw me. "Damn it. Look what you did!"

At home, after Mom put peroxide on the cut above Chris's eye, I took off my karate outfit and stuffed it in the back of the closet.

27.

I was eventually transferred to a different junior high, one that was difficult to get into because it was in an affluent part of town. There were no metal detectors like at my previous school, and students ate lunch outside. I was unprepared academically and so was put in remedial classes that took place in trailers at the far edge of the track and field. I never went. I was there on scholarship, and teachers frequently told me that my tenure was a trial. Chris, who had stopped being a Satanist at thirteen when he became a Baptist, was a senior and had recently dropped Christianity for marijuana. He picked me up every morning after my mother dropped me off at school. We smoked weed from a bong in his friend's basement.

28.

When the transfer went through, I anticipated changing my study habits, maybe working as a writer for the school newspaper. But

I'd learned different life skills at the previous middle school. I'd learned to strike first before an actual gun was pulled or before I, too, was cornered in the stairwell. I resented my new peers.

I got into a fight with a kid who'd been checking me all semester. Dogwoods bloomed just outside the stairwell window where we fought. He called me "Opey Taylor Donald Duck cluck-cluck looking like a raggedy old junked-up Vanilla Ice turkey neck donkey tooth motherfucker." I hit him first. He landed at least five punches to my temple before pushing me down a flight of stairs. I managed to make it outside to the grass before I passed out.

29.

"I can only note that the past is beautiful because one never realises an emotion at the time," begins the famous Woolf quote. "It expands later, and thus we don't have complete emotions about the present, only about the past."

30.

Eventually, Superman kills Doomsday for good. He used the Wayfarer's time-traveling bracelet and teleported the monster to the very end of time, as the galaxy collapsed in on itself, and he tossed the creature into the deadly crush. Superman returned to the comic book pages where events occurred without cycle or chronology. His death nearly forgotten but for the mistrust—a hesitancy in manner—that became a part of the Man of Steel's character from then on.

VI   My Mother Taught Me How to Be

My mother turned four in an isolation ward for polio victims, learning the language of illness before arithmetic or cursive. One morning, in the yard just beyond the kitchen window of her family farmhouse, she sifted dirt into water for mud pies. Sometime later she woke, unable to speak because of a living pain, like an infestation of fire ants through her skull and spine. The year, 1951; the polio vaccine would be made public in 1954. Confined to a wheelchair, she could not visit her family. On Sundays, nurses moved her to the window, and she waved down to her mother and father, who stood together on the sidewalk. The virus eventually passed through her system, but the damaged muscle tissue, ruined from such molecular cannibalism, would never recover. She was sent to a children's hospital in Memphis. Her parents moved from their farm to a bungalow in Midtown. After years of restricted use, her legs withered and shrank. She needed operations. The remaining muscle, skin, and bone was cut and stretched and then sutured back in place with pins and staples. There were more surgeries to come, and she would be a teenager before the last one took place. But eventually she walked.

*

An abandoned antebellum house next door to our own was torn down, and for years after, there was only mud. One summer, my father borrowed a grader and flattened a large stretch beside our property. We set up diamonds made from pillowcases filled with dirt, and my mother taught us how to play baseball. She was always the pitcher, her pole-thin legs and scissorlike walk steadying on the mound before throwing underhand to Chris or me. Amanda played outfield, sitting in the dirt with a collection of dolls in her lap. My older sister, Kim, hit home runs. The fence acted as an umpire. When the bases were loaded, which was rare, Mom would make up a name for the invisible player on first. I never questioned her ability to throw, even if she lost her balance when the knee on her weaker leg locked up. I never thought to be embarrassed by her disability. We were her children, a pack of protective wolves; we encircled her while grocery shopping, were quick to yell at an able-bodied driver who had taken the one handicapped parking space. We told men, "No thank you," when they asked if we needed help. Our mom could handle it, we knew.

*

My mother often seemed unaware of her disability. She despised unneeded attention to her weakened legs, and I recall her anger once, at the zoo, when a flock of birds with gaits identical to hers, a widened swing of the left leg and short step of the right, followed her around the aviary. My siblings and I thought it was magical. Something nonhuman had taken a shine to her, and we grew raucous, imitating the birds that followed our mother. We were oblivious to her exceedingly frantic steps as the birds closed in, wings raised, surrounding her feet. It wasn't until she cried out, her breathing shallow, that I stomped and clapped the birds away. No longer threatened, she sat down on a concrete bench—"My own children," she said. "Laughing at me, mocking me. How dare you?"

And though we apologized, remorseful, we had drawn attention to the very thing she worked so hard to disguise.

*

There was a period when my mother wrote children's stories. One is a personal essay about growing up in hospitals with poliomyelitis, written in the child's voice; another is about adoption; other stories follow rabbits and squirrels with the names of children she'd lost before my brother and I were born—twins, stillbirth. The parent rabbits try to explain the loss to their only daughter, Kimberley, but it is clear the story is more about a grieving mother.

*

When I was seven, my mother wanted me to go into the Cub Scouts, but there was no den leader. And so she volunteered. For three years, she organized lock-ins, sketch-comedy performances, and movie nights and signed our troop up for various summer camps. When I recall my mother from childhood, I often see three faces that match various phases in life: the first belongs to quick flashes of anger, the way her mouth and eyes grew hard with violence; the second is wistful, as she sat at a drafting table drawing variations of architectural remodels she imagined for the house on Meda; the third belongs to her time as my den leader, with rouged cheeks and glittering watery green eyes. When a missionary who had recently returned from Korea showed interest in the position, Scoutmaster Bud hired him and fired my mother—"It ain't right having a woman training these boys," he said.

The missionary held a sleepover at his house, and we were allowed to bring a movie of our choice. "Don't worry about bedtime," he said. "Stay up late if you want." I'd borrowed a copy of Eddie Murphy's *Delirious*, a VHS in the off-limits section of my mother's dubbed tapes. I knew it was there because I saw Mom take it off the shelf the night before; my parents' laughter, heard from my room upstairs, was as continuous and lively as speaking.

Within the first five minutes of the film, Joshua Sparks locked himself in the bathroom because he was not allowed to watch R-rated television. He cried and banged on the door because he could still hear Murphy cussing. My mother was called to pick me up near midnight, and when the new den leader said, "This really isn't appropriate for children," my mother, instead of reprimanding me, told him, "Kids already know this stuff. I don't want to shelter my boys."

On the way home, she said, "That guy is an asshole." I held my unfurled sleeping bag, pillow, and the VHS in my lap because we'd left the house so fast. I picked at the label, written in Mom's handwriting, curious now what this allowance meant. She had sided with me, even though I had taken an R-rated movie without permission, even though she had been called from bed late at night to pick me up from a sleepover. The new den leader, however, was an outsider—a man who threatened the true pack.

VII   Rock and Roll High School

Winter and I hid in the near dark behind a wicker papasan, pushing two pennies back and forth and declaring, "That's my two cents on the matter." The prismatic allure of psychedelic mushrooms had quieted, and our thoughts settled once again on life. Winter was from southern Florida and nineteen years old, and she had already hopped trains and hitchhiked out west. Her blonde hair was cut into a bowl that framed cat-eyed glasses and wide, white teeth. She didn't rent anywhere but bounced around from couch to couch. I never saw her reflective or depressed. She kept those emotions private, I assume, because I, on the other hand, held out my insecurities for all to see. At sixteen, I was officially considered independent by law, so truancy officers were kept at bay and I could work full time as a dishwasher. To replace self-doubt, I painted elaborate pictures for anyone who dared to ask about my future. I said I might live in Hawaii, eating fish from the sea and fruit from trees; I might live above a bakery in Paris; I might ride a bicycle on an Indonesian beach, carrying a pet monkey on my shoulder.

"You should come with me to Montreal," Winter said, "if you want my two cents."

I don't know whether it was the mushrooms or the ease with which Winter seemed to move through her life, but I agreed.

The following evening, I cornered my father with my plans while he bent toward the bottom of the fridge for a Dr Pepper. I had convinced myself that traveling to Montreal was the best response to dropping out of school. "Winter has friends in Canada," I told him. That's all I knew. She had acquaintances who offered her a place to stay for the summer.

He laughed and shook his head, but neither action was playful. "You're not going."

I did not know how to say I felt pathetic spending my weeks working in a damp, hot dish pit where half-eaten plates of lamb cost four hours' worth of my pay. The audacity and uncertainty of leaving *was* something, even if *something* just meant *new*. Instead of telling my father that the future frightened me now that I was a dropout and that I did not know how to invite change without pushing limits of safety, limits of comfort, limits designed by fathers, I said, "Report me as a runaway if you want, but I'm going all the same."

As I walked up Young Avenue toward Maxwell's, I heard music blaring from a car stereo somewhere in the geometry of residential streets. Muffled at first, the volume expanded as the vehicle drew closer, closing the distance—*Drove my Chevy to the levy, but the levy was dry.* Don McLean's "American Pie" is a song about loss, about the death of American icons Buddy Holly, Ritchie Valens, and the Big Bopper, but by 1997 its elegiac connections had been severed, becoming instead so commercially overused that to be heard anywhere—a grocery store, an elevator, near gas pumps as ice spindles dripped steadily into a pool of motor oil—conjured images of tanned flesh near a lake. It was a reflective song, a song about simpler times, a song that sucked away any technological anxiety of the approaching twenty-first century, and left one, momentarily, fixated on the sky.

I hated "American Pie"; no, I loved the song when I was nine years old and envisioned my sixteenth year as a summer afternoon hanging around a reservoir, swilling Coca-Cola. But as the song grew in volume, my shoelaces forever loosening and matted with grime from the dish pit, my life looked nothing like how I'd dreamed it as a preteen.

A truck pulled up beside the curb, and I kept on toward work, picking up the pace. After years of walking from place to place in Midtown, I'd grown accustomed to strange men propositioning me: "Want a ride?" "Let me touch it." "Put it in my mouth a little." When the driver honked, I recognized the sound as belonging to my father's truck even though the horn was factory installed—*toot-toot*—my ears were attuned to all subtleties surrounding him. I saw him leaning over the bench seat toward the passenger window.

"What y'think? Just put in new speakers." He tossed his aviator shades onto the dash. Relax, his eyes told me.

I mustered a half-embarrassed smile, trying to hide how uncomfortable I was standing in public with my father and Don Mclean. "Sounds good," I told him. I didn't care about stereos, or cars for that matter. My brother did. He had a trunk full of speakers and subwoofers.

"Damn right it sounds good." He turned down the stereo. "Always wanted speakers that could carry like that. We can fix up that Cutlass, you know."

That Cutlass, a 1981 baby-blue Supreme, was *my* car. My father had worked extra hours and on weekends building cabinets for a lawyer as trade. I didn't have a license. The Cutlass dimly hovered in my daily consciousness as a symbol of remorse—cobwebs around the side-view mirror, animal prints muddying the hood—and when I recalled how happy he'd looked on the day he had presented me with the gift, the memory always stung.

The entire family had just sat down for dinner.

He said, "Bring in my tool belt, will you?"

When I went out to his truck, I saw what I thought was a neighbor's car parked behind his but paid it no mind as I unlocked his passenger door, located the tool belt, and began poking around for a discarded butt. When he called my name, I looked up and saw my family standing only a few feet away. I understood then. The car was meant to be mine. I revved the engine the way Chris might've and was grateful for the smoky holler popping through holes in the muffler. I loved the pride I saw in my father's eyes as I held the steering wheel at ten and two, and in that moment, I thought I'd get into cars after all, drive down to New Orleans with friends. *I could do this*—imagining myself covered in grease.

And now, standing outside on Young Avenue in the June sun, I understood my father was trying very hard to reestablish a connection. He wanted to lure me back to the fold with youthful comforts—cars and stereos—and I loved him fiercely for this bribe. But I did not know how to give him this without also canceling my trip to Montreal.

"I'm late for work."

"Fine," he said. "See you later."

He turned up the stereo, paused briefly at the intersection, and gunned it onto Cooper Avenue.

At the Greyhound station, a few weeks later, I waited for the bus alone. I bought a ticket to Detroit, and even though I held a stack of transfer passes with gate numbers and departure times, I still asked the woman at the customer-service desk if gate 1 leaving for Nashville was actually the bus meant for Detroit. Though she never smiled, she exuded a simple kindness. I was a boy in her eyes, a boy without supervision. She told me to wait at the door so I could hear the driver call. By the time the bus arrived, my legs had gone stiff from sitting cross-legged on the linoleum. After I handed the driver my ticket, he reached to take my overloaded pack. He told me I'd have to check luggage that large; it would not fit overhead.

I ultimately traveled with it on my lap for the next thirty hours, because buried at the bottom, hidden in a sock, was the $650 I'd managed to save washing dishes.

The bus did not depart for at least twenty more minutes. From my window seat, I watched other buses pull away one by one. Men smoked alone near the terminal. A few women stood together in a cluster; one rocked an infant in a stroller. There were no other teenagers on the cusp of similar adventures. An image of a parallel sixteen-year-old driving with friends to a lake house flashed through my mind. I heard their giggles and quick moments of bickering; felt the steering wheel between my hands; and glimpsed the absurdity of my decision to travel away from home, away from my family and friends, among total strangers. By the time my bus finally pulled away from the station, I was despondent—it was the other boy, the one I'd imagined driving my Cutlass east on I-40, his friends passing a bottle of vodka in secret. I did not know where they were going, but I knew that they were on their way toward graduation, toward college, toward marriage, and that I was on a different track entirely, one that had no known destination.

At 6:00 a.m. Winter and I parked in front of a row of buildings crowded closely with first-floor bodegas and advertisements for french fries smothered in gravy and onions. Winter's friend Stephan met us at the door of the fourth-floor walk-up. Beers were opened and passed around. Other housemates awoke, and soon the kitchen had filled with people. I didn't talk. I loved listening to the floating French while sipping a bottle of Lucky and smoking next to the back door. Stephan's housemate Dom brought out a bag of PCP. I'd never snorted anything before. As I watched a telephone book and ID and straw and lines of PCP move from person to person, I thought of my parents and the cocaine Chris had found in my mother's library. Had they still been so young when I was in elementary school to get high like this? Imagining my father snorting coke with friends did not shock me—no, what made me feel ill at ease was considering their ages in this moment, an enthusiasm that no longer enveloped the house when my father came home from work. What was the pivotal moment when the cloak of youth slipped away? I thought of the look in my father's eyes just before he sped away on Young Avenue, "American Pie" blaring from his new speakers. He feared losing me, I knew. I caused him fear.

The PCP burned when it caught in my sinuses. I choked. Those close to me laughed and patted my back. The patting, of all things, embarrassed me—*It'll put hair on your chest.* Some hours later, I called my father. He answered on the first ring. "I love you, Dad," I said by way of greeting. I was trapped at a threshold between Montreal and Memphis, between father and son, and I longed to step into one place or the other. I don't remember what we talked about, nor can I place how disconnected my ramblings must have sounded. When I asked to speak to Mom, he said, "I don't think so, Son. I'll tell her you'll call tomorrow."

It was a month before I called home again, and when I did, no one answered.

Downtown, one afternoon when the temperature had spiked to over a hundred degrees, I leaned against a brick wall that edged the side of a diner, with some street punks and Winter, as they spared change. A man walked past, tall in a gray suit; he smiled and pointed toward the alley behind us.

"Ten bucks to see it. I pay."

I thought of all the men in broken-down vans and pickup trucks back home whom I'd cursed loud enough for someone to hear— *Get out of here, pervert.* I didn't need the money. My savings were still strong. For years after, I called myself an anthropologist or a coward, depending on the mood with which I told this story.

The businessman followed me into the alley and then behind a dumpster. I pulled my dick out for him to see. He said something dismissive, a disgusted, annoyed look on his face. The whole time, he was speaking French, and I had no idea what he was saying. It wasn't until he repeated the same phrase more than once that I said, "I don't speak French."

"You are pathetic," he said. "I pay to say this, boy."

The apartment on Ontario Street was unusually festive. A couple had just arrived from Paris. Winter sat next to me on a gold couch laughing easily, a laugh that inevitably ended with deep intakes of breath like geese honking. She bent into a story she was telling; her blonde bangs hanging over her eyes. In one hand was a miniature screwdriver, and her glasses were in the other, wobbly and loose. The couple from France would take our coveted spot on the floor. Winter was going to live with a man whose sky-blue eyes matched lines tattooed across his temples. I had nowhere to go, and Winter had not invited me to move with her. She passed me an airbrushed mirror—palm trees and a purple sunset—with lines of speed drawn out. I bent into the PCP. Even after weeks of getting high, I was still amazed by how easily the powder shot through, disappearing entirely, save for a thin layer of mucus that collected at the back of my throat.

Metallica's "Whiplash" broke into a guitar solo that I normally loved but was now so piercing that I took the record off, popping up the needle. I wanted something somber, and ignoring outcries, I put on the Police's *Reggatta de Blanc*—*I hope my leg don't break / walking on the moon.*

That was the last thing I remember.

When I woke up vomiting, suddenly surfacing from an abyssal sleep without any dreams, the room was steeped in further darkness. I was upright on the couch, exactly as I had been during the opening notes of "Walking on the Moon." No one was around. All lights in the apartment were off. The Police LP still rotated on the turntable, a *crrrr-ssshhh* sounding as the needle edged the paper centerpiece. I vomited into cupped hands. There was not much to release, only strings of sick. I rolled from the couch and onto my knees. I laughed, an ugly attempt to fight off crying. I had been left alone. Never had exhaustion felt so aggressive, so haunting. I stood and paced the room. I lit a cigarette; it burned against the inside of my throat. I took off my shirt and pants and stuffed them into a plastic bag that once carried beer. In the shower, I slowly released hot water until my skin reddened and the dial was all the way open.

Afterward, I dressed, putting on my shoes with laces still matted with grime from the dish pit. I thought of the new stereo speakers my father had installed in his truck—*My, my Miss American / walking on the moon.* Was this not what he expected? What if I'd been lying on my back when I vomited? I sat in the dark. I smoked, calming myself. Not feeling calm. I would ask for money to fly back. I dialed the 1-800 number on a phone card my father had given me. I wouldn't tell my father about the speed. I dialed the twenty-two-digit access code and then our ten-digit number. I would tell him. I imagined the phone ringing in my house, the cordless lost somewhere in the folds of a couch, in Amanda's room, below a cookbook in the kitchen. It rang, and I knew then that no one would answer. Night? It was night when I sat on the couch next to Winter, night when I changed out the record. *What time was it now?*

I didn't want to be alone, and so I walked to Pop's RV.

Pop was a silver-haired man so shrunken with age that it was hard to believe he lived nocturnally, driving to the far reaches of the city to feed street kids hot dogs and prepackaged cups of orange juice. He'd converted an RV into a mobile diner with tables and chairs, a hotbox, a fridge, and a microwave. He left schedules all over town with times and locations—he came to Frontenac at 2:00 a.m. People crammed into the RV. Some sat but most stood, eating hot dogs the way one drinks from a faucet, crouched and hovering below the buns. Pop said he was moving on, and I asked if I could join.

We drove into parts of the city I'd yet to see, eventually parking in a neighborhood that looked bombed out with tenements boarded up or broken open. I handed out food from behind the hotbox while Pop rested in the driver's seat. Two men and one woman, all three around twenty—lank, bruised—slid in and out of consciousness in the booth where I normally sat. I placed juices on the table, but no one pulled back the tinfoil tops.

Around 5:00 a.m. Pop dropped me off at Frontenac Station. The lights were off at Stephan's, and no one answered when I knocked. I rode the subway out near La Fontaine Park. I waded through a darkened path, holding out my lighter. I hesitated at every step until I scrambled off the main trail, kicking back brush and pushing aside limbs. I came to a large tree that was wide enough to conceal me from the path, cleared away the brush, and curled into a fetal position, digging sticks from beneath my hip and shoulder.

When I awoke, I was drenched in sweat. Sharp slashes of hot sun shot through the canopy. I had no water. I was thirsty. I crept through the woods, watching for people on the trail. I walked to a grocery store and bought cheese, lettuce, bread, fruit, and chips. I also bought a gallon of water.

For the next two nights, I camped beneath my tree. I tied food in upper branches and tired myself out walking the city during the day. In the dark, I thought of my father. Proximity, like love, like order, offered him comfort. This was a difference it seemed, one I had to reconcile as a son; the unfamiliarity of that city park in Montreal grounded me, as if before I had been filled with air. I didn't miss the ballooning—this tethered floating so near to the ground.

A week later, I flew back to Memphis from Detroit with sparse chin hair, weighing a scant 110 pounds. This flight was my first. After landing, a tarmac crew attached a small staircase to the exit door, and people gathered belongings in a great rush of clacking seat belts and rustling clothes. I looked through the window and saw my father below, shading his eyes from the sun. I had expected my mother, and seeing my father brought me to tears. I buried my face in the seat back, affecting boredom or exhaustion, but once I started crying, I could not stop. I was grateful. I recognized his love. He looked so much like himself that I questioned if anything had changed. But it had; I had. He searched the airplane windows. The aisle was full of impatient passengers; the wide thighs of a woman in leopard-print leggings hovered near my seat. When he finally caught sight of me, he smiled and waved with only his fingers, as if I had simply been returning from summer camp.

VIII   Halfway Between

I recall how heat lightning fractured night clouds. And how we huddled close, my friends and I, crouched on a pedestrian walk that paralleled the Highway 55 bridge, a rising arc over the Mississippi River. I'd jimmied an ink pen into the nickel-sized keyhole of a maintenance hatch, and when the pen slipped from my hand a third time, Grant mocked my failed attempts to turn the lock.

"Seriously, man," he said. "Give it here." He'd recently grown a beard that obscured his boyish, searching eyes, and I envied the authority this mask offered. My own face was smooth, hairless.

I tossed him the cheap Bic chewed at one end and told him to crack the fucking thing if he thought he could do better. He laughed at my temper. Bob laughed too, as did the woman he'd brought. I'd never met her before. Her name was not given. It was my last night in town before moving out west, and this, in a sense, was my going away party.

Leaving the lock to Grant, I leaned against the railing, the only thing separating me from a hundred-foot drop into the Mississippi River. Darkness fed along the embankments, but at the horizon, where the river bent south, a triangle of sky showed. On the other side of the walkway, just beyond a two-foot concrete partition, eighteen-wheelers sped across I-55. I grabbed a beer from my bag.

"Stand on the cover," Grant told Bob.

"Why, because I'm fat?" he asked. "Get Sticks to stand on it." Bob gestured in my direction. Sticks—at nineteen, I was nothing but bone. Short and cylindrical, Bob had dubbed himself Tubs, as if we were some comedy duo. He wanted me clownish.

"I'll do it," the girl said, smiling back at Bob.

With the cover pressed, the lock, a steel bar that hitched the manhole closed, slid free. The four of us stood over the square now opened in the sidewalk, a ladder descending onto the concrete platform below. I held the cover back so that it would not fall accidentally as the others climbed down. Red warning lights alerted barges of the bridge's nearing columns. The rhythm was timed, and my friends' bodies flashed in a strobe of light and shadow. The descent was my favorite moment, climbing below the sidewalk and onto the middle column beneath the I-55 bridge, halfway between Tennessee and Arkansas. I don't recall how I'd learned of its existence, but when finally below the four-lane highway, trucks rumbling ten feet overhead, the Mississippi below, it was as if I'd burrowed beneath the skin of Memphis.

Bob climbed up a second, smaller ladder onto a narrow maintenance bridge made of perforated metal with aluminum rails along each side. His friend squealed when he strolled casually onto the catwalk. I was also terrified the first time I went out there. The metal grate made it appear as if there was nothing between you and the water below. The thrill came from challenging this liminal space and returning unharmed. We were inconsequential kids from working-class families with no high school diplomas, and time was something to count as opposed to let pass over our teenager years. This understanding of the world was what brought us below the bridge. We sought the derelict, the dangerous, and the illicit as a means of belonging to aspects of the world, of Memphis, that were inaccessible and hidden from most and therefore special. This secret knowledge gave us definition.

Grant and I followed the girl. On her hands and knees, she gripped the metal, moving cautiously above the abyss. I sat beside her, my legs dangling. Below us, a barge moved through the water, and we tossed our empties onto the deck, never thinking about whether anyone was working or sleeping outside for the long haul to New Orleans.

"Y'all been caught down here?" she asked Bob.

He said he hadn't. But I remembered how earlier that winter, one night when the temperature had spiked and the air felt balmy, I had taken a date below the bridge. I'd brought cheap wine, and as soon as I'd unfurled a blanket, the wind carried it away, a blue-and-white-checkered square in an otherwise blank expanse. We drank from the bottle, sitting on the cold concrete. Not long after we'd arrived, I heard the manhole open from above. I had anticipated police, but the two guys who climbed down the ladder were in their midthirties and dressed like they'd just walked off the set from a 1980s film about heavy metal. One guy wore a flip-bill Suicidal Tendencies hat, and his friend sported an Iron Maiden do-rag. There'd always been signs of life under the bridge—names scrawled out and added together like middle school dating announcements, proof of disappeared generations that came before. The two men were as shocked to see us as we were to see them. They were polite. The one wearing a do-rag pulled out two extra beers, passing them to my date and me. He introduced himself as Peanut. His buddy, he said, was Suicidal. Suicidal quietly watched the river, holding a cigarette pinched between two metal tongs of a prosthetic arm. Suddenly, Suicidal turned to me and asked if I did pull-ups. I'd said yes, of course, though I hadn't exercised since eighth-grade gym.

"Oh, hell yeah," Peanut yelled. "Come on!"

I then watched as Peanut climbed over the platform railing, grabbed on to the base of the catwalk, and swung out above the river. I anticipated his fall, a flash of color and muted splash. I yelled for him to climb back, but Suicidal told me, "Shut up. He'll be fine." I didn't take my eyes off Peanut as he proceeded to pull up once, twice, three times, and on until ten. "It's why we come down here," Suicidal said, and he stood up, meeting his friend at the railing. We didn't stay long enough to see what happened next. My date and I quickly climbed up to the pedestrian walk and ran back to the car.

Bob's friend said I was ridiculous, and I liked her then, was glad she'd come. I loved to tell this story. Not only was it an absurd chance meeting with two men who, like me, had come below the bridge seeking meaning, but Peanut and Suicidal were proof that my personal mythology belonged to this landscape. I had witnessed. I was an active participant.

Before he spoke, I saw Bob shiver with a darkness that frequently washed over him. Call it doubt or fear or depression or all the above when mixed with whiskey and beer, but he often switched off in an instant. I chose to ignore him and settled into the silence that followed her laugh. Bob stood and shouted he could do pull-ups off the catwalk.

"Sit down," Grant said.

"You scared, Granty-poo?" Bob made a fake sad face. "Worried I'm gonna fall? You know what? I don't give a fuck."

Steel struts spanned the distance between the column and outer truss. They were higher than the catwalk. Bob managed to crawl onto one. There was no railing along the struts, and diamond-shaped holes the size of shoeboxes separated the crosshatched ties. He pranced from the column to the far end of the bridge, singing, "I don't faulking care," in an unconvincing brogue. He looked miniature against the vast backdrop—the river; the train bridge; and a little farther up the shore, a gaudy pyramid—like that blue-and-white-checkered blanket let loose in the wind.

"Walk back," Grant said. "Slowly."

Bob tiptoed toward us, each foot dropping shakily in front of the other. He lost his balance, and one leg kicked wildly as his arms flailed above his head. With an awful clarity, I imagined his body bulleting into the current below; a barge carrying him into the gulf on its bow; my hand wrapped around the brass fittings of his casket at his funeral.

Catching his balance, Bob steadied his arms. He knelt, gripping the strut tightly, knees dragging against bolt heads as he crawled toward us. Once he reached the railing, he dropped heavily onto the platform, hunched in alternating shadow and red light.

"Let's go home," he said.

I thought about home. I had begun to fear descending down from the pedestrian walk ten years later, as Peanut and Suicidal had done, with more inventive ways to challenge my limitations, until I, too, might hang dutifully above the Mississippi's powerful current. Distance was key if I ever wanted to hear what my spirit sounded like without influence.

But what if leaving home was similarly as stupid as Bob's little dance? What if I found myself in danger of falling without an aluminum rail to grab hold of, without a set of friends to watch? I knew I would go all the same. I've yet to return. Something was lost in the trade, however, something still present among childhood friends, a simple ease that comes from maintaining a connection with the streets and dangers of youth on into middle age. I have forgotten how to love one place, have not remained in one city long enough to identify with the landscape as wholly as I did with the I-55 bridge.

IX   Thirteenth Street and Failing

MEMPHIS 1998: NORTH WATKINS AND PEACH STREET

On this day, I lie the death of Wes Todell. At seventeen, I don't
have knowledge of real loss or real death to stop this lie. No one
has driven through the guardrail at the Highway 101 and Black
Lake Boulevard exit and sideswiped the orange-and-blue Public
Storage sign. I've never held the hand of a dying woman. I only
know a simple longing for attention.

Walking home from Café Society, my shirt wet around the stomach from hours of washing dishes, I stop at Peter Pan Grocery and
buy a twelve pack. I ask the clerk to bag the beer. I don't tell him
that I'm underage. By the time I arrive home, red fissures have dug
into my fingers in the shape of folds from the bag handles, and the
decision to kill Wes forms.

No one is at the rental. The message machine blinks. I hope
it's a crush, but it's only my mom. She wants to know if I need her
to bring over dinner. She says there is plenty left over. I want her
to, and it is for this reason that I don't call her back.

I walk out onto the porch and sit on the weather-beaten couch

I brought home from the alley behind the Chinese take-out place. Leonard Cohen's "Chelsea Hotel" plays from speakers set up in the open windows. I finish one beer more quickly than I should, open a second, and wonder how Leonard Cohen can make a song about a blowjob in a hotel so sad.

A couple of years back, I visited Wes in Yardley, Pennsylvania, with a mutual friend named Jack. Jack had lived near Wes in wooded suburbs next to Wolf River on the city line. Wes had only lived in Yardley for three months by the time we went up there. We told our parents we were at each other's houses for the weekend and then took a twenty-four-hour Greyhound north with a girl named Mandy. When we arrived, we learned Wes had only asked his parents if Mandy could stay. He wanted to fuck her, and his reasoning for getting us to come all that way without a place to sleep was that Mandy would have said no if she had to travel alone. Jack and I slept under a bridge, and in the morning, Wes and Mandy came down to the ravine. They had smoked sherm, and the effect left them hallucinating one minute and spaced out the next. Wes and Mandy would often forget themselves, and Mandy would stare off into space while Wes turned angry and screamed, "I hate this goddamn place." Jack and I ate our breakfast of cheese crackers and strawberry milk while Mandy went down on Wes's flaccid dick.

From the porch, I watch Grant park out front. He and three other friends, including Jack, pour out of his Toyota van. Grant asks if my mom brought over any food, and I tell him no. Bob says Leonard Cohen is depressing. On the concrete walkway, Jack repeats kickflip 180s while drinking from a forty bottle of Olde English.

About a year before this day, Wes visited Memphis from Yardley and stayed at my parents' house. He smoked crack in the bathroom. We smelled the acrid smoke seeping under the door, and he came out with a cloud rising around him—his face submerged in folds of shagged out bangs.

"What the fried chicken? I'm . . . fricasseed," he said, and his short legs visibly shook beneath a pair of forty-inch polyester cutoff pants. "Fried colonel . . . huh? Yep. Yep." His arms wiped his body as if he had just run into a spiderweb strung out across two branches. A couple of hours later, he unplugged our VCR and ran out of the house. My brother tackled him and got the VCR back. Wes ran away through the darkened neighborhood.

No one had seen or heard from him since, until this night, out on the porch, when I invite him back.

"I heard Wes died," I lie.

When anyone asks how, I withhold details with vague shrugs and make noncommittal presumptions like, "I don't know. An overdose probably." I lie that I heard secondhand so that no one questions me.

On the porch, everyone is silent as they choose how to react. The truth would be to say, "I'm sorry he's dead, but what a fucking asshole." No one seeks the truth when faced with mortality.

Everyone worries over Jack, who knew Wes the longest. Jack sits on his skateboard and rolls side to side. He searches for his own attachment to Wes's death and reels in memories. He places each memory in a different cooler until his boat is full of emotions that flap like suffocating fish out of water. There is nothing for him to do but stand up and skate off. He won't come back until late at night. The others will keep on drinking for the next two days. Some, who only met Wes once or twice, will remember their friends who committed suicide, overdosed, or died in car accidents, and they will purge these losses. And I will use the lie of Wes's death again and again. I will kill Wes for strangers. I will kill Wes with friends who never knew he existed. I will kill Wes again with those who did.

OLYMPIA 2001: PUBLIC STORAGE

I forget the last few guitar notes of a song my band Sicarii has just finished writing. When I ask if we can play it again, our drummer, Eli, reminds me that the band that practices in the space next door is waiting outside for us to finish. Even though it's March and still cold outside, I wear a T-shirt. The strap catches on my sweaty back as I place the guitar in the case. Parker, the other guitar player, practices the new melody at high volume.

Jamie, who will stop playing bass with us after this evening, slaps Parker's arm and, with a shy laugh, tells him to turn down.

We play in a Public Storage complex, which allows bands to practice. Entrance requires a code, and once in, the gate locks. We are separated entirely from the world outside, and I enjoy this aspect.

We finish practice early, so the quiet guitar-drummer duo can use the space. The singer, Emma, has a wispy voice that matches the drummer's raking brushes. The rest of the complex is empty but for my band and Emma's. Emma is only an acquaintance now, but in a few years, she will take care of my cat, Miette, while I return to Memphis and find that Wes is alive and well and living in my old neighborhood. Jack will run into him at a Laundromat, and he will cry and hug Wes. For now, we take our time removing guitars and turning off amps; we talk about the intro to the new song, reluctant to end the moment.

Then, I hear the clapping sound of a flat palm on the soft aluminum door from outside. A current of energy that does not emanate from the electrical equipment moves through the room. The knock. Emma screams; her words are indecipherable. Jamie opens the storage door, and we all exit together into the rain and cold. Emma wears a peach-colored hoodie and jeans, and her brown hair covers a face grotesquely contorted with fear. She grabs Jamie and holds him, even though they have never spoken. He does not like physical contact, but he doesn't push her away. I feel jealous, not because I am attracted to Emma, but because my role in the evolving drama has yet to be defined. It takes me a moment to find her drummer. He sits with his back against a shuttered door, his face hidden in the folds of his arms.

"What happened?" I ask.

He shakes his head, not looking up.

The air is cool, and there is clarity within the light. Shadows are sharply defined: the dip in pavement where water pools at the sewage grate and, farther up the lane, the steely flashes of cars exiting Highway 101. A torn guardrail and, below that, a green Jeep Cherokee, half-cocked against the steep hill and curved into the pole that holds the Public Storage sign. Every window, shattered.

"I'll call 911," Parker says. We do not have cells, and so he runs in search of a pay phone.

Eli and I look to each other. We communicate all that is needed in silence: neither wants to walk to the Jeep, but we won't let the other go alone. We don't run. We measure our steps toward a prevalent smell of burnt rubber and oil dripping against hot metal.

An almost perfect circle of personal effects litters the grass and paved lot around the Jeep. I see a copy of Leonard Cohen's greatest hits, and "Chelsea Hotel" runs through my head on a continuous loop—*You got away, didn't you, babe.* Highway 101 is perhaps fifty feet above me. Other drivers have stopped, getting out of their cars now to call down: *Is everyone okay?* A pair of Keds with no laces are perfectly positioned near the pedals, and through the busted windshield, I see the body of a woman past the steering wheel sprinkled with fine shards. "No," I say in response to the onlookers but not loud enough for anyone to hear.

We run to the woman, Eli and I. We move fast so that we might catch up on the time we've wasted looking in wrong places. There is no shadow here, simply light. Her brown hair has fallen across her face, but I can make out a blunt nose and the pocked scars of acne and, when she blinks, light brown eyes. Her pants are ripped down the front, and her shirt is torn away, exposing bare breasts. It is cold. I want to cover her with a blanket. We don't even have our coats.

The woman lets out a long, painful breath, the first I've heard, and then nothing. I kneel, and so does Eli. I take one of her hands, and he takes the other. "Don't talk," I tell her. The woman breathes. Then she doesn't. She has no marks, no blood, no scrapes. Eli tells her she will be okay. I think *don't die don't die don't die don't die.* Eli holds her hand too tight, and I tell him this. The woman breathes.

Then she doesn't. We hear sirens. Lights flash above the low-slung buildings. Each flash is an inversion, like flipping a light switch on and off. Sirens swell, agitating my concentration—*Shut up. Shut up and let me save her*, as if I could transfer into her dying my own vitality. The woman breathes. Then she doesn't.

A policewoman tells us to move, but we don't. I can't. I continue to hold her hand. The officer says, "Get the hell out the way so EMT can do they job."

The officer asks if we witnessed the accident. We make her nervous, I can tell. She takes my arm, holding it too tight around the muscle, and escorts me to the car. "Go home," the officer says. "Not you two," she tells the duo. "I need a statement." The guitarist still holds on to Jamie. The drummer does not look up.

PORTLAND 2002: THIRTEENTH STREET AND FAILING

I sit with five others in my attic room. New York Dolls plays on the stereo. It is not a party, but we feel festive. The rain hasn't stopped in over two weeks, and we are all eager to break our hibernation. Roughly hewn wood and tar paper separate us from the steady drum of rain. Someone puts on Leonard Cohen, which changes the mood into something somber.

There is already one empty jug of Carlo Rossi, the cheapest wine in the store, and I open the second. Passing the jug around, no one asks for a cup. This is my new room, and Portland, my new town. Three months have passed since we called the police department to see if the woman lived only to learn she did not. Emma went to the woman's funeral and learned that her name was Jane and she had two children.

Here in the attic, I fight against thinking of these details. Within the comfort of the wine, cigarette smoke, the space heater, we share stories of traveling, touring with bands, family, and friends— everyone laughs. I laugh, too, but can't concentrate. I see Jane's torn clothes, exposed. Unfocused eyes. Twitch of a finger and then nothing. Eli's breath, white smoke in the light.

I want these friends to know, but I don't say anything about the woman.

Someone tells a story about a friend who has been on the nod for two weeks. So far, this friend has managed to get kicked out of every place that has welcomed him. He left uncapped needles in someone's bed while the person was at work, passed out with a cigarette and burned a couch only to drag the smoldering cushions into the yard and then run away while everything burned.

"I had a friend like that once," I say. "I kicked him out of my house for stealing our VCR. He died soon after. Overdose."

I speak Wes's false death as easily as if it were truth, but Jane is suddenly there. I can see her Jeep. Her Keds. My lips are dry. I take a drag, and my fingers slide into the burning cherry. I can feel the policewoman's tight squeeze. My friends offer sincere apologies. They all tell stories of their own, stories of loss, of death, of friends gone awry. My lie is countered in their certain movements, intonation. I know they are telling it straight, because inside my blood, this is how I tell the story of a woman who died in a complex among strangers.

X   Memento Mori Part One

Calls in the Night

Hungover, I downed a glass of water in the kitchen of a friend's duplex, my mouth ashy and brain swollen. I tried to zero in on the wall where all my belongings were stashed, when the shadow of a man stepped onto the front porch. I heard boards creak. I listened for a knock. I figured it was a Jehovah's Witness or the landlord, people I did not want to meet. It was a weird choice staying here instead of, say, with my parents during my final days in town before driving to the Pacific Northwest. Meda Street reminded me too completely of who I'd once been, a brother and son geared in a way specific to my own malfunctions. The stranger knocked a second time, and then came a third, cop-like rapping. A silence. I peeked around the corner and saw no officer or Witness.

The house phone rang a few minutes later. Thinking nothing more of the visitor, I began a failed search for my toothbrush. It wasn't in my backpack. All I found was paste and floss. Buying a new one was tantamount to skipping a meal. I had a savings, something like twelve hundred bucks, but once in Olympia I would not have job prospects or a working knowledge of the landscape. The answering machine picked up—"I'm looking for my boy"—I was shocked to hear my father's voice. He paused. "Tell him to give me a call on my work cell."

By the time I recovered, he'd hung up. *Was there an emergency?* He sounded calm. I peered through the glass security door and saw him sitting in his truck. The engine idled. I reverted to the wide-eyed boy who was unsure of himself in relation to his father, fighting simultaneous urges to hide and bound.

I stepped onto the porch, and he waved me over. "Want to grab lunch?"

He moved a mound of invoices and a nail gun to the floorboard, and I stepped up into the passenger seat. My father looked away, tapping out a rhythm on the steering wheel. I followed his gaze. Across the street, behind a blooming magnolia, sat an abandoned house. Busted out windows were covered with plywood, but the front door was missing and the gaping interior was visible.

"Y'know, Meda didn't look much better than that dump when I bought it?"

I tried to make out his eyes behind the mirrored shades. Something in the way his mouth cast down, not moving, told me to be watchful. "Ready?" he asked, putting the truck in gear.

I grew restless on the drive to Krystal Burger, not knowing how to respond to his silence, his awkward glances. I tried—*Still on that condo downtown?*—but otherwise I kept quiet, waiting for him to make the first move. That's what adult men did; they bit back useless talk. He ordered food at the drive-through window and pulled into a spot that faced away from the main road. He placed a burger on his knee and tapped out a cigarette. I did the same. We smoked with the windows down. Though I wanted to appear cool, collected, I jumped at his every move and doubted the way my hand fell limply from the wrist. I did not know how to be an adult around my father.

"When you coming back?" he finally asked.

"Christmas, I think. I need to find a job."

"You'll just pick up and move like it's nothing?" He gripped the wheel with one hand and adjusted his weight; the muscle in his jaw worked hard. "I bounced around some too. Traveling is the easy part. Setting roots is what's hard."

I shuddered at this particular rebuke, because *setting roots* was exactly what I wanted to avoid. The thought did not conjure images of life source or stability. I measured the weight of his everyday world—up at 6:00 a.m. for a full day at work, dinner in front of the television, accidental nap in his recliner, cigarette burning out against his calloused fingers—with the weightlessness of my youthful ambitions. For my father, roots, though difficult to establish, gave his life a stable foundation on which to build. He watched me, and I watched my dwarfed reflection in his mirrored shades. What could I say, that I saw a spark in others I didn't know how to articulate in myself?

He removed his shades, set them on the dash. Then he looked at me, sizing me up. There was no longer anger in his stare. Nor was there joy. "Nothing feels right," he finally said. "I'm trying to . . . It's you taking off. And me—I've hit a brick fucking wall. Just thinking about it makes me dizzy."

"Why don't you take Mom to dinner or go out with friends. Do you have friends?"

Stuffing the burger back into the bag, my father started the truck. He mumbled about getting to work but didn't move. I stuttered out an apology, though it came off hollow because I wasn't sorry. What I meant, instead, was that I wished I'd said the right thing.

*

My father sits in the darkened living room on Meda Street, an occasional hiss of car tires passing outside on Young Avenue. The television's silent strobe. He has leaned forward in his recliner, overstuffed, very comfortable for the first fifteen minutes of sitting, but any longer and his back begins to ache, the muscles in his neck tighten. The Weather Channel scans the country, moving from the

Midsouth to the Midwest, until eventually the announcer lands on Washington State, where his younger son now lives. He doesn't know what his house looks like or if he is eating enough or if he has found work, but he learns that today, still three hours from dawn out there, Olympia will be sunny. He stubs out his cigarette, pulls his hair back from his eyes, shakes another loose, and lights up again. He should quit, he knows; that's what everyone seems to be doing these days, giving up cancer sticks. But what other pleasures does he have? He coughs, a long hacking fit that happens so frequently he rarely notices anymore. He thinks about this for a moment—*How fucked is that?* It makes him smile in a friendly way, this self-banter. It's the way he likes to talk with others, you know, giving them shit for acting in ways that ain't exactly good but ain't bad either. He'd never go after anybody for something serious, only fun teasing.

But his mind hardens just then, when he recalls in perfect detail how that red Pontiac had braked hard in front of him at a light on Summer Avenue, his fingers tensed around the steering wheel, a gash on the middle knuckle. In his mind, there formed a bleak, poisonous darkness, and his vision blurred. There was no peace in his fatigue. He needed to get out of the truck. He needed to lie down. The light changed, and he had not noticed. A car honked— the memory shifts.

Now he sees himself curled into a ball on top of the comforter, one arm resting over his face, blanketing his vision, all of his being dedicated to the simple act of drawing in breaths and exhaling, but they were shallow, short. In his mind, a total and awful absence of sound and light. His wife stood at the side of the bed and she wrung her hands and she wouldn't quit asking, "What's the matter, honey? Oh, baby, what happened?" He curled tighter, drawing his knees up to his chin—*Pull it together. Pull it the fuck together. You're not dying. You're not.* And with this memory, sitting in predawn light, his chest tightens. "Fuck me," he says out loud, trying again for levity. Beneath his ribs a pain shines as if a sharp knife is slicing his arteries. He frowns, rubs the hard cartilage of his nose. He's surprised it's never been broken, his nose. The thought of fighting and winning calms his nerves. He recalls a particular fistfight from his youth. The kid was older and bigger, and they kicked up dust in the field next to his mama's house. But he can't hold the memory very long before it's replaced by what he calls, when far removed from the attacks, the Nothing. Like that movie his kids liked to watch, the one where the black fog comes through and eats up the world. That, too, naming it, calms him. He doesn't say it aloud, the Nothing, not to anyone else—no one needs to worry over him. Soon, perhaps, but he ain't bad off enough yet.

He should make coffee, he thinks, something to add a little clatter and activity to his mind so he can look away. (Does it make a sound, the Nothing? Like a buzz, subtle and irritatingly quiet? Or is it cacophonous like an inner-city subway station built so far below the sidewalk, the escalators, rising, each step disappearing into the seam, never reaching open air? The echo of human voices and the screech of the subway coming to a stop and the distorted intercom mumbling indecipherable names and places. My father did not like crowds. In those late-night hours, did his mind feel crowded?) He thinks, again, of coffee. He cannot catch his breath and his eyes strain and his muscles tense and fingers tickle the chair arm and his toes tap inside his moccasins. Something inside him is expanding well beyond the size of his body. He is a container too small to withstand the pressure building first in his chest and then down his arms and into his fingertips. He stands up, and he suddenly cannot find the will to walk into the kitchen and dump grounds into the filter and press the goddamn ON button. He is angry now. Now he is scared. He cannot remember what set him off. Only the freezing-cold ache inside his chest. He rubs out the feeling— *Something's got to change. I can't keep this up.* He lights a cigarette and goes into the kitchen, puts on coffee.

It is still dark when he arrives at the warehouse. His crew is working on Main Street, renovating a building that probably should've been condemned with all the work that's gone into making it livable, every damn thing from the electric to the plumbing to the floors and walls. Even the roof needed to be retarred, and the foundation on one side had to be shored up with a mountain of gravel and a retaining wall. Ain't that something, he thinks; all that backbreaking labor, all those hours, and can't no one tell once it's said and done. That's the point, he guesses. Customers are supposed to walk into a renovated property and see potential, not the work, never the work; they're not supposed to think about the construction, only the finished product. It should be enough, he thinks. It used to be.

Nobody is at the warehouse, and they won't be until 7:30. But that's why he comes in early, to skip running into Todd or that other lazy son of a bitch Pat. His men are good workers, always on time, and they're nearly done with the Main Street job.

The warehouse is cool and cavernous. He likes it here, among wood stacks and piping and copper and tools; it's like his very own lumberyard. It's not his, he knows. It belongs to Todd. He couldn't deal with the customers, couldn't sniff out money the way Todd does. He used to want something like what Todd has for himself—didn't he? When he was younger, it was all about hustling up cash, what with Linda's baby girl and then Christopher? She was so scared about that boy, after she'd lost the twins—*stillbirths*, man, that tore her up—but the doctor put her in the hospital down in Memphis and monitored her last weeks. He was left in Paragould, living with his mama. He and Linda wrote to each other every day. He remembers never knowing what to say, so he just said what he'd done, little things—*Is that when I bought a pound?* He thinks so. Damn near tripled his investment. Linda was pissed off when she found out he'd been dealing drugs, even though she smoked as much as he did when she wasn't pregnant. She said she wanted honest money, and he heard her out. If she wanted her family raised right, so did he. She was still skeptical of him back then, he knows. She wasn't sure how much boy was left.

He pulls next to the gas pumps at Circle K, cuts the engine. He's so damn tired it's like he could curl up right there in the midst of all the heat and fumes. He takes off his sunglasses, tosses them on the dash. All he wants is a refill on his Big Gulp. That boy of his keeps badgering him to drink water, tells him dehydration is what makes him so tired. But hell, Coke's got water in it, and coffee does too. What does his son know anyway, to always be so damn self-righteous? If it ain't water he's on about, then it's meat or the fucking TV. *If he didn't look just like me, you'd think he was somebody else's kid.* And then he thinks of the time that he grabbed his son and shoved him through the wall of the upstairs hallway. This memory haunts him even though no one was hurt, didn't even scare the boy he's so damn ornery, but he had overstepped some line, he thinks, because when he'd shoved his son with a fist drawn, he did not see his own flesh and blood. For a while, he blamed his son, just thinking about how he mouthed off all the time, how he did whatever the hell he pleased and whenever too. Wasn't that when the boy started to pull away? He really hates to think it, but he blames himself for his son living in Washington. Farthest anybody can get from Memphis.

He gets out of his truck just when a car pulls up next to him. Two men around his age have the stereo up loud. He thinks about telling them to turn the volume down, way down, but he doesn't want to start shit. It ain't like he's got anything against the guys, but blasting music as if the whole world wants to fucking listen? He walks across the parking lot, looking back, studying the man's graying hair, his stylish clothes, and a little dance he does as he pops the nozzle into his tank. A man that old, my father thinks, and acting like a teenager.

The cashier calls to him. "Hey, Chris," she says, drawing out the simple greeting. He straightens up, walks over to the counter, smiling. He knows how and when to be charming. An employee of that same gas station for nearly ten years, this woman flirts, and he gives back, even though he doesn't find her the least bit attractive. What he likes is making her feel wanted. He's good looking, he thinks. Young enough. Forty-five isn't old.

"Leave that rap shit to the kids," he says, gesturing to the pumps. She shrugs. "I like it."

Todd is on him, yelling, first thing, "Where the hell you been?" Todd looks foolish, like a little boy who is denied cake and demands to know why. His gangly arms flap at his sides, and as he walks toward my father, a socked heel comes loose from one of his sandals. "The guys tell me you been gone since lunch," he says. "Where?"

My father has barely made it into the foyer of the downtown condo. He sees Junior, the youngest and only black man on his crew, his best carpenter, standing on a ladder and holding a piece of trim above a high window. He'd driven to the river, trying to fight down the Nothing. Todd, he knows, is putting on a show. It's not personal, or he doesn't think it is. And he struggles to find an excuse, any reason besides the truth. That he'd fallen asleep in his truck. That he hadn't been sleeping lately. He can't think of anything else, and he is angry that Todd is demanding of him something he doesn't want to give. He tells Todd he had something to take care of, something personal. He calls out to Junior, "Everything fine here?" Junior calls back that, yes, it has been.

Todd is not appeased. "I can't have my foreman gone all day. Not while the endgame is on. What if something had gone wrong?" Todd asks. "What if the owner had stopped by?"

He hears Todd's words differently than they were spoken: *Can't have his foreman gone* automatically translates into *Can't pay a lazy son of a bitch.* My father bucks. He hasn't had a reason to flare up like this in years, not at Todd, but his temper is like a spark at the gas pump. Always has been that way, and he likes feeling something that has always been and knowing that it's still true.

"I ain't the fuck off, and you know it, Todd. That's your best buddy."

Junior hammers down the trim. Ronnie cranks the chop saw, cutting angles for the window; Marky runs a bead of caulk along the finished molding.

"How many clients you brought in, Chris? How many?" Todd asks. "That 'fuck off,' as you call him, has contracted five jobs for the firm this year. Five! I'm talking money, Chris."

He'd never considered contracting jobs for the firm, and this knocks his anger down. It doesn't add up. Why was a coforeman meeting with clients? Had he known that's what was expected of him, then of course he would've struck out and brought in contracts. He was a sought-after carpenter.

He drives to Supercuts in East Memphis because he doesn't want Linda to cry while cutting his hair the way she'd done, what, over ten years ago? It had taken him nearly a year to find a new job after Dick, his old boss, had left him high and dry in the mideighties. Got so bad he even tried working fast food, but they told him he was *over*qualified, whatever the hell that means. Those were hard months, he thinks, back when the boys were in grade school and Amanda was a toddler. The house was so full with the spirit of children it was impossible to take the lack of work in stride. What good was he as a father if he couldn't provide for those babies? He didn't know if it mattered, not in construction surely, but he had cut all his hair off so that he might look more professional. Todd was impressed by his clean cowboy boots and flannel tucked into nice jeans, but Todd had no way of knowing those were his only new clothes. His long hair means something to him, means he doesn't have to conform. He works hard, pays his taxes. But he hopes the haircut might help him out of a bind a second time. If anything, it will be a change.

When the bell on the barbershop door jingles, he jumps in surprise, not because it scares him, but because it reminds him so much of home, and for a split second, he is confused. He is next in line. He sits down and fidgets with a copy of *People* magazine. All those damn celebrities look ugly to him. Tom Cruise is there, his teeth so white and perfect they look plastic. He remembers how fucked up Tom's teeth were in his earlier films. He liked those more. Same thing with the tits, not a natural pair in the whole magazine—*Who cares?* Hair doesn't mean much as long as he stays on track and gets back on solid ground—*I can look tough some other time.* This makes him laugh; the receptionist looks up from her typing. If he has to stop working with Todd, if that will help straighten him out, he will. Hair or no hair. Without thinking, he taps out a cigarette and lights it. He draws in, exhales, holding the filter between his teeth. The receptionist rushes over to him—"Sir, sir?" She is nearly frantic. "You can't smoke in here," she says. "Put it out, or I'm gonna have to ask you to leave."

He is startled by her reaction, by the implication that he is someone who needs to get kicked out of Supercuts. He apologizes, says he'll leave, and he does.

*

"Well, you got your way!" my mother said over the phone. I readily pictured her face: mouth taut, speaking through clenched teeth.

With the phone cradled to my ear, I passed by the kitchen on my way to the back porch. My bandmate Parker scooped coffee grounds into boiling water. We had very little by way of home furnishings. There was a soup pot, a few scattered dishes, and a table with only two chairs for four people.

"What right do you have, telling your father how to live? The way things been going!"

"What happened?" I asked when I reached the ratty couch stored out back. Across the alley was a typewriter repair shop with a window full of old Olympias.

"*What happened!?* You told him to quit his job! He can't quit his job," she said. "Your daddy told me, '*Y'know he's right. I need to take control over my life.*'" My mother's imitation of my father was fantastic. She stomped through her phrasings as if playing a hillbilly ogre in amateur theater. "You better set this right," she said. "It's all a mess. He don't sleep. He dozes in his recliner after dinner and then tosses and turns until 2:00 a.m. only to pop awake. Enough to drive me crazy. I get up every time he does. He won't say a damn thing—he'll listen to *you!*"

Why would I tell my father to quit his job? Or *when*, for that matter? I hadn't talked to either of them since late September. I'd been avoiding home. After two months of living in Olympia, I still hadn't found a job. I'd been lying to my father for weeks, saying I worked as a projectionist at a theater (truthfully, I volunteered as one at the Capital). I didn't have to lie. The lying briefly transformed my situation into something worth mentioning.

I called my father's cell.

"I told those fuckers I've had it," my father said, laughing. "I'm sick and tired of Pat and Todd not doing a damn thing, while I'm out busting my ass."

As superintendent, his job was to go from site to site and make sure everyone had what was needed and did good work. Some of the men, he'd worked with for years. He didn't need to police them. On this day, Pat's crew had called my father in to help fix a botched job. I never thought to ask what had gone wrong at the site, but I imagined my father huddled around a set of blueprints, pointing into the skeletal structures of rooms. I pictured him climbing a ladder and taking measurements of beams that had been cut too short. They'd have to order new lumber. All I knew was that my father worked alongside another man's crew to right whatever had gone wrong when the owner and coforeman showed up drunk.

"I walked up to Todd and told him, 'I'm quitting if you don't fire this asshole.' And you know he just stood there, looking stupid like he had nothing to say," my father said. "Kept asking me, 'What's the matter?' I told him, 'I'm waiting. It's either me or him.'"

It had taken Todd a moment to pull himself together. Perhaps he did not want to look weak, but he eventually yelled, "You got no right telling me how to run this business."

My father had gotten his answer.

"You have to work, don't you?" I asked. "I mean there's no severance if you quit?" I couldn't bring myself any closer to the subject of money.

"I'm not going back," he said.

I thought of my mother—*You got your way.* What was *my way?* I had misplaced the memory, but now I recalled a letter I'd written my father from the Badlands in South Dakota just two weeks after our interaction at Krystal Burger.

In the Badlands, after days and nights of driving and sleeping in rest areas, sharp peaks rimmed in purple and white surrounded me on all sides. The formations appeared frail yet jagged in contrast to the lifeless meadow that stretched so wide that the sky and earth blended into a continuous, two-dimensional wall.

I woke up early and set off on my own, following a narrow path through the interior, a labyrinth of sharp angles and rocky nooks until it dead-ended almost immediately into an alcove. I could see, in the distance, a green meadow at the summit of a particularly flat range. The grass and few trees floated above the rough terrain. I had nothing with me besides my journal, stuffed in the waistband of my jeans—no water bottle or snacks.

I clambered up the side of a hill, packed clay breaking loose and sliding out from beneath my feet. It was a difficult and stupid feat of endurance. Each hill was steep, and the ranges had formed so close together there was no other way forward besides climbing up and over. I was often forced to backtrack and seek a different path. My foot fell through a thin shelf that loosely bridged a wide fissure. I didn't move, my thirst rising. I had no idea how long I'd been walking. Inside the hills, I heard nothing but my labored breathing and the occasional *tink-tink* of falling pebbles.

The trees in the meadow were much too small to sit under, and the sharp grass cut into my ankles. There was no shade. From my hard-won overlook, I saw the road, a diner, and a museum. I sat on the flat edge of a boulder and decided to write my father a letter about the landscape. He needed to see something new, I reasoned, as I was doing. Routine had blinded him from the open, shocking beauty that existed in the world: "I've been thinking about your situation. I think you should make some spontaneous, senseless decisions. Live like you haven't in so many years, and life will take over for itself."

When writing these words, I was thinking of the splendor that lay before me. "Spontaneous" was the word I chose, but what I meant was that I wanted him to visit the Badlands because *he* had decided a trip might clear his mind. I wanted him to clear his mind. I'd never considered that such expanse was what he dreaded most.

*

In November I finally scored work. The Inland Worker's Union in Seattle hired me to lash trains to barges. I was placed on a list for nonmember employees. Work was never steady. Calls came the day before a "casual" was needed. But it paid fourteen bucks an hour with time and a half after eight hours, and I rarely worked less than twelve.

On my first morning, the crew waited for the trains in a one-room trailer. Until the conductor radioed in, we were asked to stay clear of the docks. Once rows of freighters were loaded onto the barge, we split into pairs and carried twenty-pound wheel locks down the aisles, dropping them next to each car along the tracks. When I'd worked for my father, I caught shit from his crew for being a small kid, a boy better built for writing than manual labor, and so to prove my mettle at the docks, I pushed myself too hard. I practically ran locks down the barge, as if this could eschew my appearance. At first, I found holding a lock in each hand to be easier than carrying one at a time, but halfway through the morning, my muscles turned to mud. By lunch I was so weak I had to cuddle the lock in my arms, braced against my stomach. For every wheel I'd secured, the other men had tackled an entire car. My partner, Aaron, weighed three hundred pounds and rarely stopped complaining. His high-pitched voice contrasted so incredibly with his body size I often flinched when he spoke—"Will you swing harder for fuck's—If our row isn't done same as everybody else's, I will throw you overboard."

At the close of the day, only Jeremy, my ride; Aaron's brother, John; and the foreman were left waiting when he and I finished. Aaron was so furious at being last that his eyes welled and he beat the bathroom door until the top hinge ripped from the frame. John caught his arms from behind and held Aaron against the wall—"Calm down, you fucking baby. Calm down."

"Aaron's got a temper," the foreman said. "Forget about it."

The docks felt familiar. I'd often pause among the train rows, my heavy breathing amplified, the Puget Sound swishing against the concrete wall separating the barge from the sea. Along the horizon, shipping cranes stretched beyond the low clouds like a herd of Cretaceous giants set to pause. Back home, I'd sought meaning in industrial landscapes like dilapidated warehouses and train yards, but working in them, instead of illegally scaling a fence, elicited a different sort of pleasure. I loved the trains, the barge, and the smell of saltwater, but I sensed a new understanding of self-preservation in the daily return to landscapes secondary to home. I often thought of my father. His work took him into antebellum houses, into skyscrapers, into rooms where he tore the plaster away, and into rooms where he disguised the construction with paint and trim; carpentry was not a means to an end but his identity. The docks, though beautiful, could not satisfy me in this way, I knew, but I began to ask what would.

My father talked to Todd and went back to work a few days after quitting. The action was like shooting road flares to signal help at a crowded intersection, and the residual uncertainty his quitting had insinuated into my family's narrative was disconcerting. Every time I talked to my mother, she stressed financial concerns. Bills were piling up, and the coming New Year would bring property taxes and Christmas. She did not mention my father, however, and when I asked her about him, she snippily told me I needed to talk to him myself. Whatever pleasure he'd derived from walking out on Todd had quickly dissipated. My mother had told me that just before he quit, my father had come home midmorning and hurried into the bedroom, slamming the french doors with such force they popped back open. Mom found Dad curled on the bed with a pillow over his face. He wouldn't respond when she'd asked, "Honey? You got a headache?" She had left him lying on top of the covers in his work clothes.

When we finally spoke after he'd gone back to work, he was reluctant to tell me the story of how he'd made amends with Todd. His boss apologized. I think this was what my father wanted, recognition.

"A stupid risk."

"Mom said you don't sleep. She said you go through spells where you won't talk to anyone. Doesn't sound like you." If some previously unturned neurological soil had triggered his actions, the way poliomyelitis had transferred from my mother's mud pie to her brainstem, a random triggering that unearthed a now nameless and unexpected reaction, chemical or genetic, then what the hell was *this* called?

"She told you about that, huh? I get headaches sometimes. I don't sleep. Two hours a night, three maybe. When the headaches come on, boy, they knock my ass out. It's just stress, Son. I can't get my mind to stop thinking. Then I get all worked up, and my adrenaline shoots through the damn roof. You won't know nothing about it—I didn't when I was your age."

*

The ILWU provided me with enough money to scrape by, and over the course of six weeks, I wrote my first novel. I worked in the condemned second-floor apartment of the house where I lived. It was a remodeled attic with a triangularly pitched ceiling. There was electricity and heat, but besides a narrow pane in the front door (it'd been condemned for not having two exits), there was only one other window, which didn't open—a rectangular piece of glass framed in the wall next to the coffee table where I often sat with an open composition book and a two-dollar sack of pens. I stared into the clouds; so low and dense, they appeared as if I could reach out and jostle an opening for the sun to shine.

An empty can of Black Label, torn in half and overflowing with cigarette butts, smoldered in front of me. I chain-smoked because it seemed appropriate to do so while thinking through plot points. I'd already written about the swing set where my protagonist, Deacon, spent his days fantasizing about escaping the trailer park where he lived with his mother and stepfather, Jon. I knew Deacon's mother had to die so that the state would take Deacon away, ultimately shuffling him into a Catholic reformatory; he would suffer abuse and eventually commit suicide. Writing the novel became a necessary escape from consistent uncertainty. By putting Deacon through the ringer, I expended anxiety, illustrating distress imaginatively so that it did not take voice in my daily life.

I worked my last shift at the docks the same week I finished writing the novel. It started to downpour eight hours into a workday that began at 3:00 a.m. All the locks had been set out, but not a single train had been lashed to the barge. I'd borrowed Aaron's extra rain gear, and all day he called me Gumby. The set was pea green, the crotch of the water-resistant pants hung down past my knees, and the rolled-up sleeves of the slicker bulged around my wrists like water floaties. He and I worked our way up from the bow. Rain fell from the hood of the slicker as I knelt, hammering a lock against the train wheel.

Once Aaron finished his half, he waited at the head of each freighter. He liked to talk about his father, a longshoreman who had died a few years before. "My diddy retired when I was a senior in high school. John had gone off to college and didn't want nothing to do with the docks. But he knocked up his girlfriend, and then they married. Fucking union gave him his card first even though I had seniority. Pisses me the hell off he got that card, but Diddy said it was on account of the baby." Aaron didn't have a family. He lived in John's basement. "Put some bite into it, Gumby," he said, holding onto the ladder of the boxcar above where I knelt. I beat the star-shaped ratchet and watched the lock nudge forward. "Why they keep calling you back is beyond me. You work about as hard as—wait, what's Gumby's horse's name? Gumby, do you know what the horse is called?"

Pokey was the name of Gumby's horse, and it both surprised and embarrassed me that I knew this information. I didn't tell Aaron. I moved on to the front wheels. With each downward swing, I had to pause, ready my force, or else I'd land a crooked, weak strike. Aaron absentmindedly stood on the ratchet I'd just secured. His weight loosened the lock.

"Damn it, Gumby. Get back over here and tighten this shit down."

"It was tight." What three-hundred-pound man is going to stomp on the lock while out to sea?

"What the fuck did you say? Come hammer this lock back down."

"You do it. You've got a hammer."

"Bullshit, Gumby! This is your side of the fucking train."

I brought the hammer down. But this time I missed, and the sharp edge of the star-shaped ratchet punched the web of skin between my middle and ring fingers. A welt of blood immediately purpled. I hopped, stomping in the gathering pools, and then in one swift, uninhibited motion, I threw my hammer at Aaron. I knew it would hit home; the aim was true. And had Aaron reacted a moment later, the ballpoint would've slammed into his ribs rather than ricocheting off the boxcar and disappearing into the muck. There was a split second when neither of us spoke. Aaron made his way toward the front of the barge screaming, "Gumby threw a hammer at me. Gumby threw his fucking hammer!"

Because of the din—silverware scraping against plates; the clatter
of glasses set down carelessly; Amanda kicking the table leg with
the heel of her bare foot, a constant *clud, clud, clud*; me chasing
peas with knife and fork—I didn't immediately notice my father's
brooding. He picked slowly at his untouched mound of mashed
potatoes. When I saw that he was not eating, I was unsure if our
mood was supposed to be festive. He stared in the direction of the
kitchen sink, the muscles in his jaw working hard. Had I missed
something with my hungry retreat into the first full meal I'd had
in months? I looked around the table. Chris and Amanda had
also taken notice. They watched him with simple expressions,
not relaxed but hidden, food slowly grinding to pulp in their
mouths. My mother sighed, a long breathy release that commu-
nicated variations of her disappointment—*It's Christmas Eve. Let's
just enjoy ourselves.*

"Get me that." My father tapped Chris's arm and pointed to
the top of the cabinets where my mother kept her collection of
decorative tin cans: Santa Claus observing an assembly line of elves,
a monkey wearing a sailor's hat and tie. My father left his hand
hanging in the air. Free of grime but for a ring of dirt beneath his
fingernails, he was dressed in a blue button-up tucked into a pair
of clean denim.

Chris stood, at a loss but eager.

My mother said, "Don't make a fuss."

"Goddamn it, Linda," my father said softly and did not continue
further. *Linda?* He never called my mother by name.

I looked beyond the table, beyond my mother, whose lips were
pursed, and into the living room. A racetrack of chasing lights
flickered against the wall. I didn't turn back until my father said
brusquely, "Bring me the damn Jack Daniels."

Chris took down a silver tin and handed it to him. It was made
to look like a bullet, and my father pulled out a quart bottle and

two shot glasses with "Old Number 7" printed on the side. He never drank. He looked the bottle over, scowling, and then set it in the center of the table.

My mother suggested we open gifts. Amanda ferried presents to each person at the table. I do not recall what I received, socks perhaps, but sitting in front of my father was the novel I'd written, wrapped in reindeer paper with soft, crumpled corners. My mother and I had spent the previous two days collating the books (she had sewn the stacked pages on her upholstery machine, and I'd glued the signatures into cardstock). He had yet to say anything at all about the undertaking. It had become a point of pride not to ask for his opinion, but I burned with expectation. The edition was small, and he was the only person besides my mother to whom I'd given a copy. I wanted to sell the other thirty or so copies before heading back to Oly. My mother had broken her last needle toward the end of the stack. I'd sewn the final signatures by hand; the pages resisted each puncture so thoroughly that my wrist shook with the force of pushing the thread through. On the title page of my father's copy, I'd written, "If you hadn't taught me about hard work I wouldn't have been able to write this book." My mother told him to go ahead, open his present.

"I'll open it tomorrow," he said, and then he asked Chris how much he thought the bottle of Jack was worth. Chris was about to offer a realistic price, but my father interjected, "Does this look like a cash bonus?"

Chris shook his head. No, it did not look like a cash bonus.

Ostensibly, everyone at the construction firm had received a commemorative Jack Daniels tin that Christmas, because according to his boss all extra funds were tied up in the expansion of his business. Todd knew my father never drank. The whiskey was a retraction of Todd's apology.

He filled two shot glasses and set them in front of Chris and me.

We waited for him to instruct us further. He stared at the bottle. Then he took a drink that ended in a coughing fit, most of the liquor spilling over his trimmed beard and clean shirt. "Shit burns," he said. "Go on and drink. I don't want this bottle here tomorrow."

After a few shots, I was drunk. My mind dulled, and I chain-smoked to keep focus.

"Merry Christmas!" My father slammed the bottle down on the table. "Fuck you! Merry Christmas! Fuck you," he pointed his finger in my face. "FUCK YOU!" he said to Chris.

"What'd I do?" Chris asked, truly indignant.

I laughed. Being around my father drunk was one of the most uncomfortable moments I'd ever spent with him, but I did not find this funny. No, the laugh was a purge of pent up nervousness.

He stood, drowsily holding on to the edge of the table. His eyes were bloodshot, and he screamed for me to stop laughing. He said I didn't know shit. Then he lost his balance and fell backward, just barely landing on his chair. Abruptly seated, he tuned out to some middle distance, and I watched as his eyes glassed over. The look seemed to ask, *Why am I sitting?*

Chris and I coached him to bed. Amanda was sprawled out on the couch, watching television with the sound off, listening to us in the other room. Our movement was slow. We stepped through the entrance hall, my father's tools piled on the floor, and into my parents' room. My mother pulled back the covers as he rolled onto his side, eyes lost again. "You two have no fucking idea," he said. "What I go through—"

"Just rest," Mom told him.

Chris and I stood in the doorway, and when neither parent said anything, we started to walk away. "Hey!" my father called after us. He propped up on a pillow. "Y'all need to go to bed." He toppled, wrapping his arm around our mother's waist. "Because, Santa Claus."

I followed Chris upstairs. Even though I would turn twenty that April, this act of slouching toward his room was worn into my physiological mapping.

Chris flopped down on his mattress. The bottom sheet had pulled away from one corner. A carburetor lay in a pan of chemical that smelled both floral and acrid; a rag on the edge of the bin dripped half into the greenish pool and half onto the floor. Neither of us talked about our father's drunkenness. We knew the self-effacement that soberly awaited him.

"What car does this go to?" I asked.

"I tell you about this girl?" Chris asked. "From the club?"

Chris had started blowing his money on lap dances. It'd been at least two years since he'd dated. During his last relationship, when he was twenty, all his front teeth had rotted without explanation. The enamel turned green and slowly deteriorated into nubs. Eating was painful, and so was brushing. And the rot hastened. Nothing hurt more than smiling. He hid his mouth behind his hands when laughing. Going to the club was a way to gain attention from beautiful women without embarrassment. But Chris met a girl who recently followed him to his car and smoked a joint; she, in six-inch heels and a sequined miniskirt covered only by a long overcoat.

"Why don't you ask her out?"

"You don't date strippers, man. As soon as she knows I'm—"

"That's the point."

"What then, man? I'm supposed to bring her here?"

Chris lit a joint. He inhaled long before passing it absent-mindedly to me. The action was as ingrained as my following him to his room, a routine developed in our early teens that was now hard to break. I declined and asked Chris if he remembered the first time he smoked me out in his car the summer before I started seventh grade. "Lightweight. Man, I thought we were busted for sure," he said. "Dad wouldn't have cared. Mom might've, but not Dad."

He said this with such certainty. That our father wouldn't have cared his two sons were stoned really pleased Chris. He saw a connection in their mutual love of pot, an irrefutable proof they were father and son. It wasn't just the weed. It was that they smoked through forty hours a week of manual labor—Chris a mechanic, our father a carpenter. Over the past few days, I frequently found them both dirtied from work—Chris on the couch and my father in his recliner—asleep with the television on.

I thought about how that night, shortly after hotboxing Chris's Impala, we went back inside and saw Dad, equally stoned, digging a pickle spear from the jar. Mom hated when anyone ate or drank from containers, and our father knew this. Naked besides underwear, with a pickle dangling from his mouth, he played up his guilt, throwing his hands in the air.

I laughed a horrid, breathless laughter and went to him out of a childlike need to be close. I hugged his waist, still in hysterics.

"What's gotten into you?"

Quickly seeing the truth redden Chris's face, I stepped away, knowing I needed to stop laughing but couldn't. To break the spell, I dove into a cartwheel that ended with my legs tied around a toppled chair. I'd turned into a kid—not the preteen criminal who'd just smoked pot for the first time but the child of twelve who could still fall into hyperactive fits.

While sitting on Chris's floor, on Christmas Eve, I could physically remember the joy I'd felt when my father held his hands in the air. It had been so long since he'd *played* with Chris and me, so much of his personality cloaked in the role of disciplinarian. Memory is all about positioning, isn't it, so that difficult experiences can easily become how we mythologize our lives. I longed to recall more instances of playfulness. The overwhelming love that had drawn me toward his embrace seemed definitively more important than anything else.

At 6:00 a.m. Amanda shook me awake. We made our way downstairs. My father sat on the edge of his bed in a red union suit, coffee in one hand, looking fresh and somehow completely free of a hangover. My mother was in the kitchen doorway. When Amanda handed out gifts, she passed him my novel. I didn't doubt he knew what it was, and when he opened it, I watched for his reaction, since I was shy about giving something I'd made instead of something store bought. It wasn't really about that; no, what made me self-conscious was how much I needed him to notice the work that had gone into the project. What pushed me to write nonstop for over a month was an understanding that this *was* work. I thought of his stamina, of all those weekend and night jobs when he had pushed himself in an effort to build a life for me and for my siblings. I had stuck with writing the book, as I told him in my inscription, because he had been my model.

My father only glanced at the cover: a diminutive demon leading a befuddled woman. I waited to see if he would read further, but he stood and dropped the book on the television console before going to the kitchen to refill his cup of coffee.

Over the next few days, the book did not move from its place on the television, and it was still there when I came home from a New Year's Eve party well after 2:00 a.m. and found my father sitting in his recliner. The lights were off; the Weather Channel played without sound. I stepped in front of the TV and picked up my father's copy.

"Your mother broke her sewing needle," he gestured toward the book.

I loved telling people how my mother had sewn the pages together. How I'd glued the signatures into the cardstock cover. Now I only wanted to hide the book. I couldn't burn it or throw it away, but I wanted to plug it into a shelf, the title squeezed out by my mother's paperback mysteries.

"You gonna read it?" I asked.

"Don't have time to read. I'll get your mother to tell me what happens."

His tongue slipped behind his bottom lip, and I saw a challenge—*Say something.* The look alone hurt more than his disregard. I didn't understand why it had to be this way. The hostility with which he stared reestablished an old boundary—You are there; I am here.

"Just figured you'd read this because—"

"I don't fucking read, okay? Got nothing to do with you. But I never enjoyed books, and I ain't gonna start now."

I tossed the book back on the television: "You got it, man."

*

My father sees clusters of tiny explosions in purple and red beneath his eyelids. Like the crown of large fireworks on New Year's Eve, the sparks sprinkle out. But now when they should dissipate, the bright motes collect into a spiral, and the funnel deepens into sound, like the roar of rapids. The noise, the extended exhale does not plateau and then fall away, not like the tide. The longer the contraction lasts, the harder his heart pumps. There is suction in his chest, as if an industrial vacuum feeds between his lungs and the underside of his ribs. The colorful lights change and draw him into a suffocating meditation. He has no thoughts. He forces his eyes open. The explosions persist, and the sucking pressure around his heart and lungs amplifies. There is a split second where he acknowledges everything in his room at once—the fireplace at the foot of his bed, the television resting on top of his dresser, the sun sifting through curtains. On his nightstand is a pack of cigarettes, and he thinks of reaching over to pull one free. His arm won't move. It's asleep; no, he can feel the blood, painfully sharp and pulsing at his elbow, at his wrists. His hands are shaking. All in a rush he sits up and the explosive colors and the sound intensify and he can no longer see the room, only a hazy, dreamlike version of things. The noises of the house sound bright, clear. Someone comes through the front door. The bells jingle, and he recognizes the stomping feet of his daughter. Amanda lets the door slam closed behind her and it booms and the bells rattle and he is startled by the hard clap even though he had been following her movements. Something inside him snaps. There is a new sound, but it lasts so briefly, like the crack-pop a residential transistor makes when a fuse blows. He jolts into convulsions, not a wild and uncontrollable seizure, but his body vibrates with such high voltage that he cannot move in any other way. "Linda," he calls from the room, but his voice is too quiet. "Linda," he calls again. "My heart."

She doesn't hear him from where she stands in the kitchen, stirring Velveeta cheese over boiled broccoli, the vegetable blanched white, but she feels that something is wrong and takes the pan from the eye. It's then she hears her name, or thinks she does. She walks briskly through the living room and into the entrance hall, where the french doors are closed, a thick curtain concealing the room where he sleeps. She hears his voice then, and so she flings open the door and finds him sprawled long ways across the bed. His legs are tied up at the bottom of the sheets. He is lying on his stomach, his face pressed into the mattress, his mouth opening and closing like a fish sucking for air. He is pale, frighteningly pale. She takes up the telephone from his nightstand, but he says no. She knew as soon as she picked up the phone to call an ambulance that he would tell her not to, and so she talks sweetly to him, coaching him to sit up. He does, slowly. His eyes are out of focus. He is elsewhere, but he follows her instructions.

At the emergency room, his wife goes inside alone, and he waits for someone to come. He can see his reflection in the side-view mirror, his face without color, his lids peeled back. His body is shaking, though he is recovering his thoughts, his sense of self, but the battering of blood does not stop. He can only repeat what he thinks to be true—*I'm dying. I'm dying. I'm dying.* He is removed from the world, everything wavering and inconsequential. An attendant meets him at the passenger door and helps him into a wheelchair. Inside, they pass through punctuated sound—every heel clap, every name called, every beep and *pssshh-sumph*—hurts him physically, like a spray of buckshot. He's placed in a quiet room on a hard examination table, and he ignores all coming or going, rubbery with fatigue. The staff doctor joins them—a young man with brown hair boyishly scooped to one side, a cowlick at the crown. He's flustered, rushing to listen to my father's heart, asking questions: "Can you feel your left arm?" "Is there pain in your chest?" To which my father answers, "I don't know." The young doctor repeats the listening procedure a second time, his movements less harried. He takes his stethoscope away, snapping it around his neck.

"Well, the good news is you're not having a heart attack. When did this start?" The doctor also wants to know if my father has taken amphetamines recently, perhaps something stronger, because he has to agree that no heart should beat that fast and hard on its own. At the accusation of being on speed, my father stands up. His movements are wobbly, and when he opens his mouth to speak, the explosions are all color again, and the funnel of sound is deafening. He collapses.

She knew what was coming as soon as that little shit with his crackerjack diploma asked about drugs. She saw it in her husband's eyes—that fire so easily sparked. Inwardly, she smiles, loving him, reaching out to touch his arm, hoping that her fingers might calm him, that her touch might make the whole thing abate, but as suddenly as he stands, he falls—a clump of hard body on the ground at her feet. She's never seen anything like it. Her husband towers briefly, and then his legs are hooked around the exam table, his face against the linoleum. "You tell me what the hell that's all about," she says.

The young doctor does not know what is happening to her husband. He says, again, "It's not a heart attack." He recommends rest and a follow up with his primary physician and, possibly, a psychiatrist.

*

I crawled into my tent, the "room" I rented for thirty-five dollars a month, leaving my shoes and pants on the living room carpet, and zipped myself into the dome. A rain guard was fastened over the moonroof for further privacy, and I burrowed happily into my mummy bag. The house was freezing; a poorly stocked woodstove,

the only heat source for a two-story bungalow. I tried to work myself
into a meditative zone, lying on my back so that sleep might come,
but I was too jacked up on coffee and still cold from the long February walk home from work.

It was past 3:00 a.m. when the phone rang. I did not want to
get out of my sleeping bag, but I knew it was for me. My father's
late-night calls had become commonplace. I unzipped the tent
and then slid like a worm out onto the living room floor. Refusing
to abandon the warm cocoon, I crawled to the chair next to the
telephone.

"I didn't think you'd answer," my father said.

"I'm awake."

I heard the unmistakable click of his Zippo, and he inhaled, deep.
He was settling in, and I, too, lit a cigarette, cradling the receiver
in the crook of my shoulder. The flame blinded me in the dark.

"It's fine," my father said. "But you'll need to come home. I'm
gonna start my own firm. Chris and you can be my apprentices. It'll
be good for you. I can have my own thing. You know? Less stress.
When I retire, you and your brother will have a thriving business.
I won't be able to pay much at first—"

As he talked about his plans, I heard genuine need in his voice.
He was asking me for a favor that I would not be able to give. I had
moved far from the possibility of dedicating myself to a Father and
Sons Construction Firm. My band, Sicarii, had a West Coast tour
booked, and a label had reached out to us about pressing a record. I
leaned back into the torn and terribly hard chair. A blue glow from
the streetlamp projected bare limbs against the wood paneling. I
drew a breath, steeling myself. "I can't." I paused, waiting to see if
he'd interject. "I know it's hard—this band, playing music. This is
what I want, and it takes all of my time and energy. I wouldn't be
able to tour if I worked forty hours a week—"

I thought about our first show back in July and how just before
we played, I'd called home, my mind tunneling through dark
premonitions. This happened frequently—a bubbling fear from

deep within my self-absorption, and I would need to hear his voice. That night, I walked from the house show to Rib Eye Diner and dialed Meda from a payphone. No one answered. I returned to the show and busied myself carrying equipment inside the dim basement lit only by strings of red-and-blue-colored lights, so dark that I tripped on something small—an extension cord, perhaps— and lurched forward clutching my guitar amp to my stomach as I fought for balance. My father anxiety steadily vibrated beneath nervousness. There had been thirty or forty people bumming around, waiting for the show to start, a steady buzz of voices, of laughter and occasional yelling, a rise and fall of speech. As Eli tightened his snare drum and I tuned my guitar, the complex tension within subsided, and thoughts of my father ceased entirely. Halfway through our first song, I looked out and saw people dancing shoulder to shoulder. Energized, I jumped during a breakdown, and though I did not get much air, a few inches perhaps, I hit the correct note when I found my feet. Then I tripped backward and stepped directly onto the off switch of the power strip. Everything went silent except for Eli's drumming. The colored lights dropped away; our amps fizzled.

"You got your own thing going on," my father said, and I snapped to attention. "But I could teach you a lot. And it'd be nice, y'know?"

"I know."

"Think about it, will you?"

"Of course."

"I had a dream," my father said. "You were getting carted out of a grocery store by the police. You stole cheese and tried to run, but they shoved you into a white van."

It was early 2002. Bush Jr. was ramping up his War on Terror. I was an activist. After 9/11 I believed more in radical change. I wanted a people's revolution; everyone I knew did. The Bush administration wanted revolution of a different kind, and every act of protest was now redefined as potential terrorism. My father's dream fed into our fantasy motifs of FBI wiretaps: Homeland highlighting our names on security lists, agents shooting photos of us from within white vans. "Everybody's on edge since 9/11."

"You're not listening to me," he said. "I can't dream. I don't. Not anymore. The therapist tells me to try and visualize things. He says I need to turn my anxiety into a beast or some shit and slay it. I can't see things in my mind. Not since the panic attacks started."

The panic attacks were the whole reason why he called under the cover of night. I was not a daily witness—not like my mother or brother or younger sister—and therefore safer than most. He had few places to turn for support. I wanted to listen. I had never experienced such an intense shutdown, an electric and painful full-body panic the way my father suffered, but I had developed a peculiar stamina for physical strain and psychic deprivation. This was nothing compared to my father's panic. What, if not from his own choosing, made a forty-six-year-old man hide in his room with the lights off? What made sound, any sound, too abrasive? There had been bloodwork and x-rays and various pharmaceuticals. My mother made appointments. She forced him out of bed and into the bath. But after one particular meeting with his primary, when the wait in the lobby proved too much for him and he suffered another public non–heart attack, attack, he refused to go inside until his name had been called. They bought walkie-talkies, and my mother would wait in the psychiatrist's lobby, in the general practitioner's lobby, in the lobby of Methodist before his appointed PET scan or MRI. My father would sit in the van, with the seat turned back, sunglasses on, and the windows rolled up. He'd been administered a cocktail of antianxiety medications, sleep aids, and antidepressants and talk therapy, until finally a name was given to his state—Panic—and with a name came treatment and, for my father, hope.

"Picture a dragon," he said.

I immediately conjured Smaug from the animated *Hobbit.*

"You got it?" he asked.

"Yeah."

"I can't do that," he said.

What would I do without my mental picture show, constant and mostly favorable? I typically *saw* what I wanted or needed before actualizing it—what does the mind do without illustration? I pictured a cave with only my father's voice echoing. Perhaps, without visual clues there were still physical sensations? Like the cold, sharp touch of a stalagmite in the dark. Mental visions were now crowded out by his panic, the panic of coming panic, not to mention the chemical reactions caused by a myriad of psychopharmaceuticals. I asked him what the doctors thought. Was he getting better? I wanted to know if the panic would always be with him inside that cave.

"Can't get anyone to believe me. You know? Not really. They think I'm just making all this shit up. Like I'm fucking *lazy!*"

"You don't believe that? They just don't know how to help. I don't know how to help."

"How could you help when you're way the hell out there?" he asked. But he quickly took it back, "I know you got things going on. I just wanted to say be careful. That's all."

He fell into a hacking fit. When he recovered, he said, "Weather Channel says it's gonna rain for the next ten days." He laughed. The joke was on me. I'd chosen to live in a depressing winter climate.

"It rains for seven months straight," I said. Fueling his banter. I could give that much.

*

March 2002. He doesn't tell Todd or his crew that he's coming back to work, but two weeks have passed since his last spell, the longest stretch of time without a panic attack since early October. The Xanax helps, but the antidepressants made him sick. The chemicals in his brain didn't mix well with whatever is in those little pills, and so he quit taking them. This morning he wakes as he normally does at 4:00 a.m. and decides to take a bath. He combs his hair and puts on work clothes. He's given up on sleep, even gotten used to the night. There's peace at three and four in the morning, an absence of things, which he finds nice. It just isn't like him to not be in the thick of things—*Busy. Confident. That's who I am.*

He hasn't seen Todd since his primary wrote up a recommended sick leave and filed it with the company insurance. Todd didn't come visit, just called once to try to cajole a specific time he'd return to work. On the drive out to Germantown, he thinks about that, Todd not visiting him in all that time. They used to be close enough. They were never buddy-buddy. He has a hard time being that way with folks, socializing regular. It doesn't make sense to him how people hook up, how he might find friends again. He needs it, he knows. His therapist says so; his son, too. He knows work and he knows family—*Ain't that enough? Ain't it supposed to be?* He thinks of his two sons—one in Washington and the other, his oldest boy, settling down with a woman and her baby girl, buying a house and making do—*They're gone. Not a damn one wants anything to do with their mama or me.*

Sometimes his thoughts bring him low, as though his conscious self is crude oil emptying down into his stomach. He tries to smile, but the sludge is too heavy. He never thought he'd grow so burdened. Not him. His wife says people light up when they see him walk into a room. That's how she puts it, as if he is full of electricity and can turn the lamp on in a stranger's eyes. That woman loves him so much that she says it still, even though what he sees in the eyes of others is mostly pity.

He stops off at McDonald's and buys breakfast for the crew.

When he gets there, the food is still hot, and three pickups are parked out front of a commercial property. He tells himself to be happy. He wants to look it, too, and when he steps out of his truck, he squares his shoulders and stands up straight. The door is unlocked, and he pushes his way into the empty and spacious storefront.

"Get back to work," he yells, before gauging anyone's reaction to his presence. He laughs a little too hard, but it's genuine. He's just nervous. No one makes a sound. It's so damn quiet. He sees

Junior, Ronnie, and that squirrely guy with no front teeth—Marky? Junior offers a funny little smile. None of the others look at him. He notices this directly. Each man busies himself. He's pissed now. Now he's apologetic, because he knows they don't know what to say. Lost his nerve, they think, and then had to sit in bed. He hates even thinking the word panic, because it makes his mind hum like a goddamn wind farm, and when the humming starts, there isn't much he can do. Anxiety is a word that splits apart and reveals little minions working at his heart, stoking his blood until it runs hot like a derrick syphoning up all that decay from long before. He said to his primary, "So you're telling me I got a sickness, and it's life?" Doc didn't find that funny: "Panic attacks are a serious disorder. Have you considered joining a support group?" Even with knowing that others also felt the blind dizziness, the spirit cold draining, it still took him months to control what was now a part of him. Like his wife living with the effects of polio, he, too, is disadvantaged. Of course, these men wouldn't know what the hell to do with him.

He sets the bags of food down on plywood screwed to a set of sawhorses and says, "Come eat before it gets cold." He winks at Junior so that he knows there are no hard feelings, and he says, "Where you want me today, Boss?"

This makes the men smile; a little joking around goes a long way. They still keep a distance, watching what they say. He feels dizzy but reminds himself he's stronger than the Nothing. He knows that now, but seeing the men turn away, well, it's like having to relearn everything about the world, about himself, always with consideration to that darkness—*A Xanax can't hurt a bit.*

"Look," he finally says, catching the men off guard, "I've had a shit year, but I'm back. Same as I was before I got sick, so can we just move on for fuck's sake?" His voice rises at the end, and it sounds like anger. But he's not mad, just needs to be heard. "I ain't gonna snap," he says, "and hurt you for looking me in the eye, and I ain't gonna whimper like a puppy if you got a problem. If any one of you degenerate motherfuckers thinks you can take me, let's have it out now. I'll whip your ass from here to Sunday if that's what it'll take." He got through to the crew. He can tell by the way each man seems to open his mouth half-full of sausage and egg and let fly a steady stream of stupid chatter.

Junior calls my father over to the blueprints, shows him the job. No fine woodwork, no frills—just walls, floor, electricity, and plumbing. He is grateful for this connection, a simple kindness, and yet the Nothing is there beneath the sleepy spell of Xanax. "Put me wherever you see fit," he tells Junior. "Just need to go piss."

When he comes out of the bathroom, after swallowing another Xanax, Todd is there. Both men are shocked to see one another. He calls my father outside, and they sit in the cab of Todd's brand new F-250. Todd wants to know if he can trust him, again.

My father tells him, "Yes, you can."

"Let Junior manage this one," Todd says. "Just until things settle a little. It's been a hard winter without you, but shit's finally calmed down."

My father straddles a plank of wood that runs between two sets of scaffolding built up to a height of fifteen feet. Before him sit three two-by-twelve lengths of pine he's just bolted together. Used to be, in high-ceilinged churches like this one, that whole trees, milled and planed smooth, were cut to the necessary size and that the timbers were connected in a grid of mortise and tenon carved out to the exact proportions and secured with wooden pegs. Twenty or more people hauled each section upright using ropes and pulleys. This inspired him, not just the necessary precision of craftsmanship, but because a timber-framed church entirely yielded to the interconnectedness of every piece of lumber involved. The work took most of the community to construct. Perhaps beams were left exposed back then because whenever the community looked up in prayer, they saw not just the craftsmanship or the promise of heaven but also their own strength reflected back.

My father calls for a fifteen-minute break. Hanging the fake beams is laborious, and the conditions—raising all that ungainly weight above your head and bolting it to the ceiling—might make any carpenter lose his nerve. They've been at it all morning, and they're nearly done, just the one left. He doesn't want anyone on his crew getting stupid because they need rest.

As he climbs down, scaling the outer scaffolding, he feels a sharp pain—hot, electrified jabs in his neck and down his arms. He knows what a pulled muscle feels like, but there's something different about this pain. He steps through the double doors of the chapel and out into the sun. It's spring. He pulls a cigarette from his pack with his teeth and lights it, and willing the sharp pains away, he closes his eyes and rests his hand on the truck's hood. The metal is hot to the touch, but the air is cool, drawing out little bumps all down his forearm. He breathes deep and the pain smarts; he breathes shallow and the pain is quieter than before. Perhaps it's nothing, he thinks. He is less hopeful than he is fed up, less foolish under the circumstances than he is afraid to face another medical leave. There's a cherry tree with white blossoms and just beyond that a pink dogwood. He tries to focus on the colors. He thinks he might call his son in Washington and tell him about the blue sky uncut by jet streams. Bet it's still gray there, he'll say.

Back inside, he doesn't tell his coworkers of his pain. There is, after all, only one beam left to bolt into place, and then the exhausting work will be out of the way. He knows he'd be mad as hell if one of his employees continued to work through an injury, but he can't bear to appear weak, not after missing so much work. Instead, he tells the men that when this last beam is up, they should take off early. The other two men climb the scaffolding with more energy than before. My father climbs slowly, feeling out how each upward reach plays on the pain in his neck. When he is finally on top of the scaffolding, he thinks he sees disgust in Marky's eyes. He doesn't wait for the kid to say or do a thing but lifts his end of the fake beam and tells Marky to scoot out to center position. Surprisingly, holding up his end does not cause him pain. But he knows the majority of the weight is still inert on Ronnie's side. With the beam resting on his shoulder, both hands clasped to the wood, my father tells the men to lift. They know the drill. Each man holds one-third. Now that the beam is over their heads, tensions rise instantaneously. At first, the beam wobbles, swaying wildly as they work to press it against the ceiling. When they have it steadied, Ronnie notices that it's crooked. My father's muscles are shaking as they work to line the beam up with the chalk lines they'd meticulously measured and marked off earlier. The pressure is making all three men take short breaths, their faces reddening. "Get your bolts, Ronnie," my father yells. Ronnie, who has wisely kept the bolts in his mouth, now clumsily drops them to the unfinished concrete floor below. Marky takes his hands away from the center of the beam in order to grab spare bolts from his tool belt. In the split second that follows, before the beam plummets sideways to the ground, my father is left holding half the weight. When recalling this exact moment later, the two men will swear they heard my father's spinal discs rupture. It can't be true. By the time Marky took his hands away, the discs in my father's neck had already herniated.

*

The police wore riot gear and carried shatterproof shields. They lined the sidewalks to protect real estate. I shuffled face-to-face with officers, their eyes obscured by a cloudy sky reflected in face guards. This day was not a repeat of the World Trade Organization protest in 1999 but a May Day march in Olympia (a small city with only two one-way streets running through downtown), a march commemorating the labor strikes and eventual Haymarket Massacre of 1886 that won us the eight-hour workday. There was tension. The police sensed it, as did the marchers. Talk of war provided this extra charge. The majority of hand-painted signs read, "Terror Is Not Defeated with Terror!" This more than antiglobalization signs—"NAFTA kills!" May Day is not an antiwar demonstration. The National Labor March of 1886 was meant to secure power in otherwise powerless situations. With no regulation on the workday, the overall structure kept laborers impoverished financially, as well as intellectually. If you didn't like it—*Fine, you're fired.*

Two weeks after suffering slipped discs in his spine, my father himself was fired without severance, without insurance, and without dignity, at the very moment he most needed compassion. He hated unions, hated the idea of dues and seniority, but if he were part of a union, Todd would never have chosen to save money by removing my father from the company insurance. My father had no medical coverage while healing from his neck injury. When I considered that I was marching in memory of unions that struck for safer working conditions, higher wages, and the eight-hour day, my father's circumstances seemed even crueler.

Eli, the drummer for Sicarii, a Vermonter with a yellow mohawk and sleeveless cowboy shirt, walked behind me. "I'm getting out of here," I mouthed. He nodded. We were set to play a clandestine show in front of the courthouse, and he was supposed to go with me to move the van to the location just before the marchers arrived. But I wanted out of the parade now: a woman of perhaps twenty, with blue hair and a bright-green tutu skipped past me, singing "This Land Is Our Land"; to my left, a couple in their sixties each carried a child on their shoulders, beaming with pride; and lined up in front of me were anarchists with black clothes and black kerchiefs walking militaristically along the edges of the crowd. I could not disassociate my father's predicament from the march. And though the marchers did so out of compassion, in hopeful solidarity with U.S. laborers whose employment had been shipped overseas, as well as for third-world workers who have no living wages or eight-hour workdays, and though they were willing to risk arrest, I only saw the cream of middle-class leisure. I saw the sons and daughters of lawyers and doctors and landlords and developers and pharmacologists and politicians. My family had no beneficent relatives, no interest-gaining CDs or Apple stock. Now that my father had been fired, my family was without a net. If I was stricken by this sense of powerlessness, then how must he feel? His neck too damaged to perform physical labor. His labor our only asset.

At the van, parked behind a McDonald's, I smoked and waited. The band had recently bought the van collectively; the loft bed we'd built before our first tour—Vancouver, British Columbia, to San Jose—still smelled of sawdust. The LP would be ready when our U.S. tour began that July. Heartened by the record, by our solid reception in California, Sicarii had seemed impenetrable before my father's news—*What does a slipped disc even look like?* Little jelly sacks between bones. I could no longer trust my optimism.

Soon the demonstrators were more than a mere hum in the air. The sound grew closer, amorphous, lovely as an ocean.

"Let's go," Eli said, appearing suddenly at the passenger door.

A preplanned human barricade blocked street entrances. We pulled onto Plum and parked in the far lane. Unloaded our musical equipment and a generator. Quickly set up our amps and speaker cabinets. A circle formed at the intersection where the courthouse, police station, and McDonald's all met. I watched officers try to push through, but they could not get to us. It would later be noted in Seattle newspapers that numbers of marchers were considerably higher in Olympia. A photo of Sicarii playing made front-page news on the Post-Intelligencer. Our band name was misspelled in print—Sickari—but the energy captured by the photographer is apparent. I'm not in the picture. I'm off to the side, out of frame. Eli's drumsticks are raised, and he is smiling. Parker's and Tammy's mouths are open, screaming into microphones. We barely have standing room, because the demonstrators are so close. I recall feeling embarrassed, flippant, when someone stopped me on the street a couple of days later to show me the newspaper. She'd been carrying it around, she said, waiting to run into one of us. I took the paper from her and mailed it home that day.

*

The wide garage-style door of his storage unit is open, and my father sits on a wooden stool, staring past the weedy alley at the large chunk of chain-link security fence that has been cut away. Beyond the fence is an empty lot where he can see a dead raccoon bloating in the sun. The fence is supposed to keep crime out, keep his tools safe, but chain link is no match for a motivated thief. Nothing, thankfully, has been taken from his space. Not yet. He doesn't plan on staying long, just until he can get his new business off the ground, but the pain in his neck, chronic and ever present, has a tendency to spike and then seize, forcing him to wait, nearly immobilized until the spasm ends. Sometimes he can't walk, his legs tingling as if they've fallen asleep. His arms do the same. "Wait at least six weeks before going back to work," his former primary told him. But that doctor stopped seeing him when Todd pulled his insurance. *Fired me like I'm nothing.* Todd bought him two weeks' worth of chiropractic adjustments and then put him out on the curb like worn furniture. *After fifteen years, son of a bitch tells me I'm a liability.* He is now jobless and in debt up to his freaking eyeballs and, following the spinal injury, is in constant, irrevocable pain. He needs more time to heal before trying to work, he knows, but he also needs to kick up some money to pay a steady doctor. He applied for Medicaid, but because the only proof of income came from last year—almost a full salary, minus a couple of months when his panic attacks were most severe—they say he isn't eligible. His latest doctor at the health department suggested he apply for permanent disability—*And that fucker, man, he looked so damn proud of himself when he said this, like it was the easiest thing in the world to just up and quit on life altogether, like all I'm after is a free ride. Told him, "Go fuck yourself."*

He knows he's done, at least for now. Inside, he feels nothing, no anger or sadness or remorse or cracking laughter. The reality is he can feel the end like a heavy breath. Everything over the last year has led to this moment, circumstantial or not, and he knows it. If his head had been right, he wouldn't have used up his savings when he was out of work—*Wouldn't've been out of work in the first fucking place.* He's got nothing to live on besides his wife's social security—a pittance of $545 a month—and that doesn't even cover household expenses. But the worst thing, what makes time the thing that chases him down, is that the city won't let him go another year without paying back taxes on his house. Two years, that's all the city gives before they snap it all up, and with the neighborhood booming the way it is—*Property taxes doubled in the last five years. DOUBLED!*—they won't hesitate kicking him out and putting the house on the market. He bought it outright. No mortgage. He wants to be angry, but he knows the game, always has. The house on Meda cost eighteen grand in '83. Now it's worth well over a hundred. The house has always been his, and yet he'll have to fight to keep it. He doesn't have a fight in him, he thinks. The pain has taken it away. The panic attacks linger beneath Xanax. It's just so damn cruel that he feels as if it's all happening to someone else.

He pushes himself off the stool, and with this simple movement, his neck contracts. He braces himself, waiting for the tremor to stop. His arms are raised away from his sides, paused in the action of standing; his knees are bent, legs spread a little. His face reddens with the effort of supporting himself. And then the spasm ceases, and all the blood flushes from his face and fingers and toes. He's pale and nearly collapses with exhaustion, a weakened sense of all things besides the white sun and the muscles in his jaw, the joints of his knuckles. He draws a deep breath, anticipating the pain that will undoubtedly follow, and, with all his will power, grasps the latch of the garage door and draws it down.

*

Days away from our U.S. tour, the record plant made a mistake when they pressed ours LPs. One side had been plated at forty-five RPMs, and the other side, at thirty-three and third. And because the record was mastered to press at forty-five, there was an imperceptible drag on the other side. The plant gave our label three hundred of the bad batch while they made a new lacquer. That meant we had to scrounge up three hundred LP jackets. We asked Kay Records and Kill Rock Stars and a plethora of other start-up labels and eventually scored enough free covers to package our LP. With my limited knowledge of screen printing, I burned a simple tracing of the actual cover—a line drawing of a ship. Our housemates helped us through the scramble. A team took turns spray-painting the appropriated covers black, laying them out in the sun to dry. When they no longer felt tacky, I printed the ship and band name in red.

Later that night, from my room, I listened to my housemates— the fluctuation of volume, tone, and laughter, before a sudden silence. I hadn't heard the phone ring but immediately recognized the concentrated absence of sound. Then there were footsteps outside my door—Eli said, "It's your dad."

My father had a proposition that involved all of Sicarii.

"I want y'all to consider moving into the house on Meda."

He and my mother wanted to move to Birdsong, Tennessee. Some years before, he'd bought a single-wide trailer. There had been a fire before he owned it, and no amount of cleaning seemed to get rid of the smell. In his voice, I heard a buried weariness. My first reaction was to agree. I was not wedded to Olympia, though I'd come to feel as protective of the town as I had once felt isolated. Sicarii was what mattered. I told him that I'd talk to the others but that it was also a crazy time for us.

"Can we revisit the idea in Memphis?"

"When will you be through?" he asked.

"About three weeks."

"What's taking you so long?"

"California. Nevada. New Mexico. Louisiana. Arkansas."

I drove into predawn dark halfway through Oklahoma. The land was flat and the van quiet. Yellow dividing lines shot past the driver's side tires and reflected upward across the windshield. Bugs splattered there too. I was jittery with the awful combination of gas station coffee and exhaustion. There had been a deep shift in weather since leaving New Mexico, where I'd worn a hoodie and a jacket, but the farther east we drove, the heat intensified. I thought about taking over Meda Street. The possibility of renting from my father had gotten buried beneath the hustle to leave for tour. Then we were on the road, unloading our gear, setting up in a basement or a living room or a coffee shop, and then driving to a new city to do it all again. The night before, in Albuquerque, I'd broached the subject of moving to Memphis, and Sicarii was skeptical. When we toured, we toured as an Olympia band. I begrudgingly belonged to Cascadia, to Mount Rainier, and to the Puget Sound. Yet I was of both worlds. I missed the South. I'd expected adventure out west, but the safe and clean neighborhoods of Olympia were tame. I couldn't recall a single intersection in Memphis that remotely resembled downtown Oly. In Midtown, gangs and cops and poverty and wealth and punks and laborers and blacks and whites were visibly mixed block by block and this collaging was integral to the city's mythology. I'd grown to expect a bright, steely tension from walking to the corner market. I identified with this uncertainty. I missed sultry summer nights, faces of friends and lovers covered in sweat. Memphis had a different personality in the small hours, a campy attitude (e.g., Memphis Queen, Proud Mary). And sometimes a mild breeze would blow steady and strong up from the river and reach into your clothes, lick your face, and the feeling, so much like fucking, would force one's eyes to close involuntarily. Memphis was pure sex in memory: cigarettes and alcohol and piercingly loud rock and roll at 3:00 a.m. Memphis was more *Wild West* than the West Coast. It was frustrating to realize a lot of what I'd sought had already existed down south. I'd changed in not readily under-standable ways since leaving Memphis. The South had become a place I'd left behind. I was more at home, intellectually speaking, in Olympia, and yet Memphis, the landscape, the people, and my family were as necessary to my life's blood as drinking water.

When we finally arrived, I went to the grocery store with my mother while my bandmates rested from the drive. I still had not slept. As she and I walked slowly down various aisles, I noticed she deliberated for long periods before placing half the items back on the shelf. Anything that couldn't stretch for a few meals was deemed excessive. She paid with food stamps. I waited until we were outside before I asked her about the EBT card.

"Your father doesn't know," she said. For almost thirty years, every week, he'd given her his check to pay bills and deal with household expenses.

"It's that bad?" I asked.

"Oh, honey, it's worse."

I stood beside her in the parking lot, waiting as she grabbed on to the armrest and hoisted herself into the driver's seat. She started the car but didn't drive away. I recalled my own penniless hunger and the food bank during those first months in Oly. My parents should not be here at this point of destitution. I'd never considered that the house might be lost permanently. His request wasn't as simple as *wanting to move to Birdsong* while collecting rent from us; it was now clear that my father had no other choice.

"Taxes. We owe thousands. There's no money to pay them outright. Look in the back," she said. "I drew it up yesterday."

Sitting on the seat was a large cardboard sign with For Sale written in marker. I hadn't noticed it before. No one would respond to a handwritten sign, I thought. Then I turned to her; she was serious about selling the house. "Your daddy could really use the quiet. Maybe that's what he needs, y'know? To get better?"

I sat with my father and mother in front of the television during dinner. The rest of Sicarii had spread out, reading or simply waiting in various spare rooms in the house until it was time to drive to the show. Amanda was at work. Chris had bought a house a few blocks away. He'd been elusive, spending his free time navigating family life. The television made me stir crazy. If I stood up to go to the bathroom or use the phone, my father promptly asked if I was getting ready to leave. I wanted to, as he expected. I needed air, and so I withdrew to the porch. I was surprised to find that it was storming out, yet the sun shone brightly over the street and yard. Beautiful. Rain poured. Everything was cast in yellow. My father stepped onto the porch. He appeared shockingly fragile these days, gaunt with a matte complexion, and he held himself unsteadily, as if the slightest gust of wind might fell him like a poorly rooted tree. There was a hesitancy to his manner, a shyness that made him, for all his height and build, look small. "What you doing out here?"

"What'd they say about your neck?" I surprised myself by asking him directly. There was no need to pretend anymore. Our many phone conversations had leveled the barriers—father to son—that had always stood between us; I knew too much now. I knew he was suffering, knew the emotional pain was more burdensome than physical, but as a simple kindness, I chose not to ask about his panic attacks. Addressing those bleak blackouts would embarrass him.

"I won't get better," he said. "Mom told you about the house?"

I nodded.

"You ask your friends?'

"I told them to consider it."

He wouldn't ask me to choose, not again. His pride wouldn't allow for another rejection by one of the few people bound to show loyalty.

A young developer passed by and noticed my mother's homemade For Sale sign. According to her, the developer knocked on the door and asked for my father by name. Apparently, he'd done his research. His offer was fifty thousand dollars. My father countered but still sold Meda markedly lower than what property was going for at the time.

After Sicarii's first U.S. tour, in October 2002, I flew home to help pack up the house. My parents were eager to be done with the city. Until they'd sold the house, even though he was still on a cocktail of anxiety and antidepression medications, he'd grown increasingly paranoid in addition to the heart attack–like panic. At night, sometimes around three or four in the morning, he'd drive to the ratty part of town where he kept his shop, because of a threatening sensation that he was, in that very moment, getting robbed. He bought a gun with the first installment from selling the house and a right-to-carry permit. One night, he actually caught someone trying to break into his storage space, but the mere sight of his truck driving up the alley was enough to chase the thief away. He waited until sunrise, the gun in his lap, but no one returned. On the drive home, he decided to buy beer, tour the city. His solitude didn't startle me; it was that he went out into the world armed, searching for something—a release, perhaps. At least in Birdsong, with a little money from the house, they could relax.

For me, it was different. I was the son who left, after all, the boy who packed a bag and tramped back and forth across the country in place of stability, but what grounded my wanderlust was the belief that I was never too far from my childhood home, my loving parents. And though I had no right to lament the loss of Meda, the act of boxing it all up or throwing it all out or driving it to Goodwill made me keenly aware that the home I'd been fleeing was the very foundation that allowed me to run.

The accumulative artifacts of my existence—love letters, photos, journals, and books—had been safely stored in the closet of my old bedroom. And I, a man who was proud to own little, to need little, found that I did not want to let anything go. When my mother asked me to clear out my things, I was somewhat surprised, having honestly believed my neglected mementos would travel with them. The trailer in Birdsong was narrow, no bigger than perhaps two of the main rooms at Meda. Almost nothing could travel with them, and my mother, a woman who covered every square inch with stuff, seemed to accept the coming loss. I recall standing upstairs, in her empty library. I figured she had boxed the books up already, but when I asked her, she shook her head—"I gave them all to the used bookstore. Some boys came and carried them out for me, so that's worth something. A lot actually." If my mother could get rid of her books, I could let go of my sentimental things, I thought. While combing through these boxes, I found the first short story I'd ever written, "The Bloody Tricycle." It was about a sister who had ridden her brother's Big Wheel without his permission and was abducted. A bloody handprint was all that remained of the girl. I'd sat for an entire afternoon in the upstairs hallway writing this story. I was perhaps nine or ten. I deliberated but ultimately stuffed the story into a black garbage bag, and so went three notebooks of poems about angels wrestling demons and losing, about cutting, about underwear models. All were set out on the curb.

Where was my father during this week of frenzied packing? I can only recall one moment spent with him, and it had nothing to do with the house. We were both awake, late at night, smoking while the television was turned to weather, the sound muted. I assumed he was comforted by the weather, a void, a place where the landscape appeared colorful and two dimensional without actual setting or people, a place where one could think without losing any time. At one point he turned to me and said—"I married your mother because I wanted someone to take care of. Her, I wanted to take care of her. To be a man she could trust."

He paused for a moment, but I interrupted his thought. "It's hard. All of it, but you'll—"

He scoffed, a gesture as familiar as his love. He shook his head in disgust, an exaggerated move meant to show me just how far from the mark I'd been. "You don't know shit. Think you do, but you haven't got a fucking clue about me or anything else. I love you, Son, but you don't."

I waited to feel the gut punch that generally followed hurtful words, but it never came. He was right. "I know," I said. "But at least I'm trying." When I said it, *at least I'm trying*, I wasn't thinking about my father at all but instead about how inside out the move made me feel now that my life, all my choices, was without the simple foundation of home. As soon as it came out of my mouth, I knew it could be misconstrued as a dirty jab, a comment meant to dig into the depths of his depression. But it was out there, a challenge, or rather an accusation.

"You can go to bed anytime," he said.

"Too bad I don't have to listen to you," I said. Jokes were our oldest language for love.

*

He travels alone to Birdsong with a notion to work. The trailer is small, but with a few adjustments, he thinks, they can manage. The bathroom, he can't stand. It's narrow as a closet, with piss-yellow linoleum. The toilet has sunken into the rotting subfloor, and the bathtub and shower were pulled out long before he bought the thing. *A fire in the tub?* His guess, someone had been cooking meth. The shifty joker who sold him the trailer couldn't have been older than fifty, but he was toothless and wrinkled. And he'd refused to take anything other than twenty-five hundred bucks in cash. Back when he was working and everything was riding smooth, a splurge of a couple of thousand dollars was doable with a little scrimping and saving, especially for a weekend home. But the damn thing was never supposed to be permanent, just shelter from the rain and snow and sun while they skipped out on the city for a night or two. What bothers him most is the smell of fire, a toxic stench like smoldering plastic. The work is a no-brainer. But the pain in his neck, damn keeling pinch locks in on him, makes everything go hazy—just one vertebrae away from being paralyzed. He should be thankful, he knows. But he's not. Fuck no, he's not thankful. He's not paralyzed, either.

The walls need to come out, then the toilet and subfloor. He's got an old central heating unit that works just fine. He thinks he can run the ductwork through the wall. It'll be a tight fit, but with just him and Linda, they can manage. When the kids come up for Christmas, that'll be a different story.

He knocks a hole in the wall with a minisledge, and then another, strategically—four corners and then a couple in the center—until the whole thing collapses. Dust and cottony fibers from the insulation fly around the room, dimming the overhead light, an awful fluorescent tube behind frosted plastic. The room, in some fucked up way, he thinks, is beautiful now. How many people witness something like this, the bathroom walls fallen in as if a tornado ripped right through the house. And yet it's not a disaster but a step toward improvement, destruction for the sake of bettering his surroundings.

As he drives the back roads toward the little town twenty minutes away from his home—*Is this what it is now, home?*—he notices that the leaves have started to change, the purple black gum and rusted-orange of maple. Country living. It's the dream, after all. He imagined it different than this—older, at least, with a pension and a list of hobbies. He needs a hobby. Maybe he can make cabinets and furniture, as he always wanted. A doe leaps from the road and into the forest. This makes him smile, and for the first time he wishes someone had come with him. His younger boy was back in Memphis helping Linda pack up the house. He should've asked him to come, but the truth is he didn't want to ask. It's hard looking that damn kid in the eye sometimes, so full of expectation. Chris, his older son, he ain't like that. He's sturdy, got his mind on the prize. Knows how to work, how to save his money, and it's paying off. The other, though—*I didn't raise him to act like that, to demand so much from the world. We're humble folk from humble folk. We work hard, raise a family, and don't cheat. And that damn kid is a thief and dreamer with not one intention of getting a job or settling down.* The boy is just like his granddaddy.

The connection between his errant father and equally absent son is out there now, swirling around the truck cab, mixing with the fall breeze, the side-slanted sunshine, and that feeling, like a hollow bubble surfacing through water, invites a kind of sadness that hurts physically. He can't bring his son home because his son doesn't want to come back. Just like his own daddy, his younger son inherited some gene that put wings on his back. He ain't no man at all, but a fucking coward. Selfish. His daddy, Jo John, must look old, if he's still alive. He's confusing the two men now, he thinks, and the hatred he feels for his son scares him.

Off exit 126, six miles west of Birdsong, is a truck stop with a Subway and an Arby's, and he's hungry. He takes the back roads, and when he emerges from the dense forest and onto a small highway just before the truck stop, he notices a neon sign: DUNDEE'S. It's a stout, windowless building. The name, Dundee, he knows it, or he thinks he does. Back when he used to party, after Linda had him move down to Memphis—wasn't nothing happening for them in Paragould besides his mama. He loved local wrestling, ate that shit up, and he went so much that eventually he started hanging out at the bars where wrestlers like Lawler and Dundee drank. They were rowdy, fun men. But that was so damn long ago. He recalls he used to perm his hair, but he can't picture himself that way now, all frizzed out and smelling like a chemical plant.

He isn't sure if the strip club belongs to Bill Dundee or not, but a last name like that is unique to West Tennessee. Hell, if he recalls, it ain't even Bill's real name, but a town in Scotland. That's right, he thinks; Dundee is Scottish. Or Australian? He pushes his way into a small entrance with a podium stationed just before a velvet curtain. Skynyrd's "Free Bird" plays so damn loud he can feel it in his bowels. There's a sign that says it costs fifteen dollars to enter, and because no one is around, he reconsiders, thinks he ought to grab a roast beef sandwich and head back to the trailer. He's having a good day, painwise, even though he wore himself out tearing up the bathroom. It's funny how shy he feels standing at the threshold of a titty bar. He hasn't watched porn but once or twice. Besides the occasional flesh shots on Showtime, the only naked woman he's seen in almost thirty years is Linda. And he thinks it should stay that way, as he stands there not leaving. The curtain opens, and out walks a stocky man with dark feathered hair.

"What's up, mate?" he says, with a slight accent. "Waiting long?" My father tells him who he is. Dundee remembers him. Or so he says. He invites my father in, waving the door fee, and they sit at the end of the bar. The club is dark with a small stage in the center of the room and little tables and chairs that look half the size of normal ones. A woman wearing high heels and a bikini walks by the only other customer, an old man, his eyes nearly hidden behind withered skin, and she lets her fingers run across his shoulder. She leans down and says something in his ear, and my father gets it now—the tables are low so that when one of the girls walks by, her pussy is at eye level and when she leans in to talk, her cleavage damn near falls across your forehead. He shakes his head, laughs to himself. "That'll open a man's wallet," he says to Dundee.

Dundee laughs, raises his shoulders—"Lucy's pussy is like a reverse ATM."

He cautiously turns back; though he doesn't want to consider Lucy's body, he feels obliged to play the part. He sees her, not the tables this time. The skin of her torso is taught, lean all the way up to a pair of silicone Cs. Dundee passes him a beer, rattling on about people my father doesn't recall, names that don't register in his memory, but he doesn't say so. He wants Dundee to talk without breath about a city and a life he has only occasionally experienced, because in this moment he isn't afraid.

Dundee says he's got some work to do. "Stick around," he says. "Have another beer. I'll be back in twenty, thirty minutes."

My father takes the beer and lights a cigarette and watches the TV above the bar—Tiger Woods, golf—as if this were a regular thing. "American Pie" comes on the PA, and he sings along under his breath. He can see his face in the mirror, without much color—too much time inside—and his hair, cut short, is gray. *Fuck it. We age. Todd will age. Dundee will age.* He feels content with this, knowing he has aged. Too soon, perhaps. And then Lucy is there, her hand on his shoulder and her tits hugging his elbow, the skin rubbery against his bicep. He can see she's young, twenty-two maybe, with acne scars covered by a pound of makeup. Her eyes are more black than brown. "Buy me a drink," she demands. And he tells her he's just here to visit an old friend, not to mess with women his daughter's age.

"You must've had her young," she says. "You don't look old enough to be someone's daddy."

At this, he laughs. Did she use it on that withered potato back there? "Listen, darling," he says, "I'm just here to talk to Dundee." She takes her arm away, her tits too, brusque now.

"Only faggots come to a titty bar to talk to men," she says, and walks off. Her heels clack, and her bathing suit bottom steadily rises into the pinch of her ass. He laughs.

Dundee is there, standing beside him, nonplussed. "The girls work the room. They flirt you up, and you let them rub all over you. Some give head," Dundee says. "But I don't know nothing about that, right? That's what this place is. Now old pal or not, if you can't respect the hustle, then I got to ask you to leave."

She's just trying to get by. He gets it now.

"Hey, listen," he says to Dundee, pulling a fifty from his wallet. "Give her this for me, will you?" Dundee waves Lucy over. Her arms are crossed, hiding her breasts.

"Take my friend here to the back room."

But my father has already stood from the barstool, an unlit cigarette hanging from his mouth, and it's there again, a total lack of fear. "You keep the money," he says to the girl. "Buy something nice. Go out someplace you wouldn't normally."

*

"Every journey conceals another journey within its lines: the path not taken and the forgotten angle." Hib was reading by headlamp from Winterson's *Sexing the Cherry*, to a group of twenty people resting shoulder to shoulder in sleeping bags on the floor. I asked her to repeat the sentence. I was moved by the idea of "forgotten angles." This was one of my last nights in Olympia, and I wasn't sure I'd made the right decision to leave this complicated, loving community of people.

Beyond the blue halo surrounding Hib's face, there was only darkness, the smell of unwashed bodies. On one side of where I lay, a couple giggled and whispered. On my other side, a stranger's hand suddenly reached out and grabbed hold of mine, and I saw sweat on his face. I had not seen him in the evening's chaos, and I would not see him the next day. The touch sought to deepen the closeness of our bodies. It was like speech, the way newly acquainted people tell stories about themselves so that they are known: *I am here*, his hand said. *You are*, my touch returned.

The house had been unoccupied for over a decade, and the owner lived in Florida. Parker and others had researched many properties in Olympia before settling on this bungalow with three feet of dead grass growing in the front yard and back, paint peeling from interior walls, and the remnants of a family's life abandoned to vandalism and the urban wilds. I helped prepare for the action, bagging up garbage. There was furniture that we used to manufacture the feeling of home. We scrubbed the appliances and sinks and tub and floors, painted a few walls, mowed the yard, and opened the windows to let in sun and air. We took before and after pictures that illustrated the stark contrast between dilapidation and domesticity. The photos gave credence to our motives—here is a house rotting from disuse, when those who need homes could act as caretakers. The direct action went on for four nights, and we slept and cooked in the house, waiting for the Floridian owner to demand our removal. It was necessary for the police and owner to get involved. Resistance like this needs to happen publicly.

I thought of my father, of my old neighborhood and house in Memphis. In the early 1980s when he bought our home on Meda, most houses were vacant nearby. There was a used-car dealership and a Chinese restaurant on the corner of Cooper and Young, and then for a time, there were only empty buildings. Todd's company and, more importantly, my father renovated most of the neighborhood as part of urban-renewal efforts, building a gringo-style Mexican restaurant and then a bank, until eventually a concrete gazebo was installed on the corner. With renewal came higher-income families and higher property taxes. Without realizing it, my father's efforts toward fixing up our home on Meda and his skill as a carpenter caused the eventual loss of the family home.

"Every journey conceals another journey," Hib began again.

The resonation of this line startled even more on second listen, but in a new direction. My mind circled two journeys: one ending and one yet to come.

My decision to move to Oakland and enroll at Laney College had been made rashly three weeks before. I had bought a train ticket and paid November's rent on a room off Telegraph Avenue. Accustomed to my own ambivalence, I made sure any way out of this move would at least cost me monetarily. A long transitional period had ended when Sicarii broke up after our fourth tour. Together, we'd traveled Mexico and Canada and the United States and driven up and down I-5 so many times that specific gas stations, boring homogenous pumps with piped Muzak, were imbued with nostalgia. It's rare for people to orbit one another permanently, especially band members, and the magic yielded. When we came together for a show, there was a restless distraction in the ways we approached one another. Band practice was often canceled, and eventually a month passed, and then two, without us getting together. This was the surface journey with Sicarii, the situation and not the story; the story was a romance. Sicarii had once been in love, had once sought to meld our personal desires to each other's fate.

*

October 2003. The sheets and blankets on my bed were the last of my things not stored or packed to travel with me to Oakland. Toothbrush and paste, loose on top of my acoustic guitar. I liked where I'd been living, a sunroom meant for plants or sitting during the dreary Washington winter. When my father called, I was lying on my back, shaking from neck to toe as I tried to reach my tenth abdominal crunch. I was winded when I answered, hiding my pant with a faked cough.

"Couldn't have picked a better time to call, huh? You coughing like that," my father said. "Listen, Son. You got to cut that smoking shit out. I'm serious. Your mom and I did; haven't had a cigarette in five days. Doctor said first three are the worst. Damn right! I couldn't look at your sister or your mama—had to stay outside the whole time."

My father laughed. His tone was pitched decibels higher than normal. I wanted to know if everything was all right, so unexpected was this news.

"I'm fine. Fine. Just time for change is all." *Time for change* was his go-to response when he needed to hide that something had gone awry, like when he cut his hair after losing his job. Or when he quit smoking weed just before the panic attacks ramped up. That day, he said he was tired of feeling like shit all the time.

"You sound funny. No offense, but it's freaking me out."

"I feel that way too. You ever quit? Out of control."

I'd been trying to quit off and on since moving to Olympia, but I'd rarely made it more than a month. At the time, entering what I hoped to be my "health phase," I'd been cutting way back, gearing up to quit again when I reached Oakland. With this thought, I realized I hadn't told my parents about the move. I'd decided to leave on the fly, scrambling to find work and a place to live: "I've got important news."

He went quiet, listening. I launched into my spiel about when I'd decided to leave Oly and why it had slipped my mind to tell them about the move. "Shit! I thought it was gonna be bad news. That's great," he said. "Always hated you living in all that rain. Get you some sun, Son. Out in Cal-i-forn-i-a. What you gonna study?"

"Literature." I was apprehensive still. Was he getting better?

Was the level of energy proof that even though the previous few years had been unimaginably difficult for my parents, now, living in Birdsong, it had, in a sense, been for the best? I wanted so damn bad to relax into this new nonsmoking mood my father had conjured and trust the coming years.

"That's great, man. Just great. But your mama would kick your ass if you—"

In the background, I heard my mother: "He's moving? Where's he moving to now?"

"I admire you, Son. It's hard work making it on your own. Just know that, okay. I love you. I tell you I bought a guitar?" Just like that, he changed the subject. "It's on the way. Got it off an infomercial for a hundred bucks. That's an okay deal, right?"

"Yeah, of course it's a good deal," I said. "I'll send you a ballad songbook I never use."

"I picture myself sitting out back picking and singing songs. I need something like that. You know? Something new to do with my hands. Dundee knows a guy who gives lessons. Always wanted to learn, and I hate the idea of never getting the chance."

XI

Memento Mori Part Two

Jackson General

I

My room in Oakland was new to me, but the brown carpet had long since flattened in a mat of spilt bong water and beer, a gift from the previous tenant, a University of California, Davis, dropout from Marin County who, when moving out, tossed his box spring over a chain-link fence directly across from the flat. The walls were baby blue, nicotine waxing downward from the ceiling. I sat in a large patch of sunshine on a twin-sized bed—my only furniture, borrowed at that—and pretended to myself that it was okay to be alone on Christmas Day for the third year in a row. Last Christmas, at least, my friend Grant from Memphis, who also moved to Washington, stayed in Olympia, and we drank until closing time. We then went back to his basement room and told each other how nice it was to be far from the place where we'd been raised. Distance still felt like freedom or, rather, a choice.

I stood up from the bed and walked to the kitchen, passing through the narrow hallway lined with closed doors. Nothing to eat. Back in my room, I picked up *Crime and Punishment* and reentered Raskolnikov's mind as he wallowed, facing the back of a sofa. His failures mixed in the chill room, but no amount of tugging on his overcoat comforted or warmed him. I knew this moment—hunger and cold obscuring a more idealized vision of oneself. Dostoyevsky was not on the reading list for my upcoming rhetoric course, but this was my first time returning to school since dropping out in junior high. I was filled with anxiety, and the only way to fight this emotion was to read. I'd always loved reading, not to mention the joy inherent in admiring the artifact, the book, once plugged into a shelf. Here, in Oakland, there were few, but in time, as with most rooms, books would spill over onto the crusted carpet and become hazardous in the night.

I had read perhaps fifty pages when both the Yemini mosque on the corner of Telegraph and Thirty-First called prayer and the hallway telephone erupted simultaneously. None of my three housemates were home, and I had not talked to my family since Thanksgiving. My father had been too weak to answer, and my mother was preoccupied with worry. But as was their way, neither ever let on that the situation was direr than a stubborn cold in need of antibiotics. Still, I did not answer right away but waited for the answering machine to pick up, leaning against the railing that partitioned the hallway from the front stairs.

It was my mother: "You need to come home. You're daddy—he isn't. Just pick up."

I froze. Her voice was uncharacteristically tremulous, and I knew without knowing that everything in our lives had just shifted. I'd been expecting this phone call for years now. *You're daddy—he isn't.* I gripped the banister and, noticing that the carpet ended a half inch from the spindles, climbed down three and then six steps to investigate the hardwood beneath, pulling up the rancid ends of carpet, ripping it free of tacks until I was satisfied that, yes, beneath was all hardwood flooring. My mind and heart ran on two different tracks—the former erratic and fearful, thinking of ways to be and ways not to be all at once, while the muscle inside my chest pumped as if constrained, the way I always imagined a drowning heart to react, attempting to tear free rather than allow water to fill the lungs.

The cordless rang a second time. I picked up immediately.

"Oh, baby," she said. I was always *baby* or *honey* or simply *Matt* or—if I really fucked up—*Matthew Randal.* But she did not continue, and the *Oh, baby* resounded as an importuning yyyy-yyyy-yyy, until I could no longer wait: "What's happened?"

"Will you come?" she finally asked.

I pushed against her tears, telling myself she was overreacting, telling her I would visit once he was well. It was rare for people to die from pneumonia. He was only forty-eight after all. He didn't want everyone crowding him, I said. When I finished, there was only silence on the other end. I couldn't breathe. "Say something!" I heard white noise. "Are you there?" I moved as a boy separated from his mother in a department store might, in tight circles, ready to scream her name but still ashamed of being *lost.*

"Matt," my aunt, my father's sister who worked as a nurse, said, "you'll need to come home. Like, today if you can. In the morning if you have to, but your daddy might not make it much longer than that, okay?" This *okay* calmed my nerves. "Okay," I said with total resolution, until I recalled the cash I kept in my hiking pack—four hundred dollars, no bank account or credit card. Four hundred dollars in a sock in a giant bag filled with everything I'd brought to the bay as a would-be student. "I need to borrow money."

I called airlines directly and eventually found an affordable ticket, but only after telling the representative why I was desperate— *You're daddy—he isn't.* I cried, and I apologized for crying. And she said, "I'm not supposed to do this, but there is a seat open on a 6:00 a.m. flight, business class."

I did not know what to do with my body. I paced, revolving in the same tight circles. Below me the carpet scratched my bare feet, the fibers long since coated by other, more durable agents. I pulled the carpet near the stairs where I'd originally peaked below, and then again. And then a third time, until a four-foot section came free in my hands, torn as easily as an old T-shirt. I tried to put the patch of carpet back into place, but defying proportional logic, it no longer fit and curled at the ends. My father was in the hospital. I had not thought the word *dying* without quickly replacing it with language that beat back terror—*sick*.

I needed to walk.

Ever since I was old enough to know freedom on my own terms, walking gifted perspective. I thought, often, of who I was. This question was elastic. I set out toward downtown Oakland with the hope that a deli in Chinatown that sold a $1.50 banh mi was still open. Laney, where I'd enrolled, was close by, and I thought I might walk around the campus to catch a feel for the environment. I liked the walk too. Leaving the Yemini corner, businesses turned Ethiopian and then Korean, until downtown surfaced and the Fox Theater's dome appeared among stretches of closely placed stoplights that changed the night into something urban and awake. It was after dark, and I had hours to fill before my flight to Memphis. The same question repeated, even when I felt certain: Why am I here, in California, and not with my family?

I could not pinpoint when separation became definitive, but I rarely went through my days without wondering why my need for independence acted simultaneously as an occlusion from home. I did not run from abuse or neglect; I did not run from anything. Instead, I was running *for* something. I regarded my father highly, and yet I was not cut out for a life of manual labor. From the age of nine or ten, I wanted to be an artist, and he responded to this with unabashed frustration, because in his experience he felt judged by intellectuals. He'd known these people, of course, known their homes and what they ate for breakfast; as a carpenter, he was invited into the lives of others who could afford bathroom renovations and two-car garages and kitchen cabinets. Growing up as a carpenter's son, I experienced this as well. Once, when I was seven and out of school with the flu and my mother was working, my father asked if I could rest in the guest room of a brick mansion while he finished building dormers in the attic. I got a crush on one of the family's daughters who was at least five years older. She liked me, too, or liked caring for a sick boy, but when we were caught talking, the mother called her into the hallway and did not close the door. "Don't get caught up with white trash," the woman said. "These men are here to work and nothing more." The daughter never returned to see me, and I never told this to my father, not because I thought he would have cared. As far as I knew, we were proud of being white trash. My father called himself a hippy redneck, and both parents did not trust professionals: lawyers were liars, doctors were crooks, and teachers were lazy. None of these qualified as an honest trade, not like "working for your money."

We were wild, my parents and us four children, living in a ram-shackle two-story house in Midtown. My father had long hair and tattoos, and they listened to music late into the night with their friends. The sound of laughing and storytelling put me to sleep, and when the downstairs was silent, I felt worried by this absence of life. Friends who stayed the night were often never allowed to sleep over again. Cigarette smoke and rated-R television were given as reasons why, but mostly it was my fault. I wanted to impress my friends with lost-boys wildness, and I'd take it too far by forcing a kid to climb on the roof or to walk around the block in the only neighborhood I knew but where two murders had happened by the time I'd turned twelve. This loss of friendship rarely bothered me, because I had my brother and sisters and mother and father. We all shared the same Pippi Longstocking syndrome, and this is what made us family.

In Memphis, the sidewalk outside the arrivals area at the airport was empty save for a bored baggage attendant. I shucked my denim jacket, held it between my knees, and dug out a hooded pullover from the one backpack I'd brought. The smells of my daily life and unwashed cotton comforted me. I buttoned my jacket over the hoodie but shivered still. With no visible sun, the moisture in the air hardened into microscopic crystals announcing a coming turn in weather. The windows and lampposts of the Memphis International Airport were decorated with red and green and white, colors so cleverly associated with gifts and meals and family that they inspired a sense of hope.

Soon Chris arrived, rolled down his tinted windows, and lifted his chin—"Let's go."

We drove east away from the city where we'd grown up, away from the Mississippi River and our childhood home, and on toward an unfamiliar town—Jackson, Tennessee—where our father now lay unconscious in a county hospital. Once on I-40, we passed a Walmart, Bellevue Baptist Church, and a long stretch of car lots, and when the interstate opened into neat rows of pitch pine, Chris lit a half-smoked joint left boldly in the ashtray. He turned on the heat; a faint smell of gasoline filtered through the vents.

"I was there when Dad collapsed," he said. "At the hospital."

"Panic attack?"

"I thought so at first," Chris said. "But he looked so pale, and then he screamed, 'Everybody leave!' He just fell. The monitor flatlined. Nurses came."

Our father had had a heart attack. Resuscitation had taken five minutes. It was the first I'd heard of his heart failure. I rolled down my window, letting in a rush of cold air, and tried to comprehend how the body and the mind sustained itself without that reliably belabored organ. I sensed my blood more acutely, a tap-tap throbbing at the base of my skull. I was not prepared for what this meant. My lungs suddenly filled with the weighted chill of too much oxygen. "Now?" I asked Chris. "Now is he okay?"

At my question, Chris began to cry. His eyes were half-hidden below a billed skullcap. Car grease stained his fingertips under the nails. The stereo played. I cannot remember the song, only the bass running through my balls as Chris inhaled the final pinch off his joint. I needed him. He was three and half years older, not many years by some accounts—my sister Kim has eleven years on me—but enough to have made him exotically beyond my grasp while growing up. I'd followed his every move from the moment I could walk until I turned sixteen and began looking for my own way in the world, a search for identity that Chris didn't undergo. He knew what he wanted, and at an early age, he began waiting for it to all fall in place. During his lean years, when love seemed hopeless, he sought comfort through smoking weed. Now he dedicated himself to raising his girlfriend's daughter. He had always been forward-thinking, if not completely adverse to anything that complicated his desire for simplicity. I, on the other hand, wanted too many things. I was open to the world and easily swayed, and yet I feared domesticity. When this split became obvious, our sibling connection floundered, and often when I visited Memphis, hanging out together was awkward in the way of distant relatives. I knew him. He hadn't changed. Instead, I was always changing, and I feared letting him know this about me.

An hour later Chris and I arrived at the hospital, an imposing structure with brown stains dripping from window units and down the outer facade. My father was in that building somewhere, and he might not come out alive. I was grateful for the time it took to circle upward through the gumball-machine curves of the parking garage, rising higher and higher—How many of these cars transported other frightened children anticipating the death of a father?

We parked. I did not want to be the first to leave the truck. Chris stared forward, not making an effort to speak. I lit a cigarette. I'd been smoke-free for nearly two months. "You know Dad quit back in October?" I said.

Chris cut the stereo, and the heavy, all-encompassing bass lingered as vibration. How odd that Dad contracted pneumonia directly after quitting. This act should've upped his immune system instead of weakening it, but I think that our bodies like addiction, that our organs and lungs get used to the abuse and ache.

My mother appeared just beyond the glass automatic doors. Shrunken beneath my father's work coat, her four-foot-ten frame looked fragile, but her anguish was unmistakably fierce. She focused on taking steps, one short and one long. She did not anticipate meeting us at this moment. When my mother caught sight of Chris and me, her face crumpled. She opened her mouth, but no words came. I did not move to her fast enough; she opened her arms and waved me forward.

"He won't look at me. I talk to him and beg him to give me some sign he can hear, but he doesn't," she said. "So many stupid movies. I thought my voice could wake him."

I didn't ask her to explain. Her eyes were icy with the bright impossibility of miracles. To say "I thought my voice could wake him" invited something like prayer: *Prove me wrong. You always prove me wrong when I have doubts.*

Not long after I arrived, my little sister, Amanda, stumbled up the sidewalk with a guy around my age, early twenties, who wore a starched cap cocked over one eye and an oversized coat, baggy pants, and shoes with laces purposefully untied. He looked like a toddler dressed up by a fashion photographer. Amanda talked without pause about how the baby gangster had offered to drive the eighty miles back to Birdsong to grab anything Mom might need. "Do you need anything? Can I take your debit card for gas and food? Can I buy some smokes—HA HA!—that way I won't have to bum yours all the time—HA HA HA!"

She reeked of weed, and in Amanda's eyes there was another high mixed in.

"Why do you need Mom's debit card?"

"None of your business."

My mother held up her hands. Her lips were pursed. "Let it be between me and her."

"When're you coming back?" I asked Amanda, but she was gone.

I searched for elevators within the labyrinthine hallways deep and skyless as underground tunnels and actively denied the severity of my father's condition. The endless rows of fluorescent tubing and fibrous tile and the stinging scent of isopropyl did not stop my mind from wandering back to Oakland, to the wall-length windows, to People's Park and Chinatown, to the course load that existed only as codes on a spreadsheet at the time but offered promise. I did not readily question my father's fate. He was alive; he would live.

When I stepped off the elevator, a floor nurse approached and held up both hands to block my path; she was sharp boned, with a slight curtain of skin shivering below her chin.

"Who are you here to see?"

When I told her who I was, she said, "Your father is stable, but all anyone can do is wait for the EEG report. Then we can know if he has suffered lasting brain damage."

Why had I not considered this—*brain damage?* In my haste to register the stats—not a panic attack but heart failure, check; still living but unconscious, check—I thought of him as being in a coma, dreaming. The heart pumps blood not only through the entire body but also to the brain. Blood carries oxygen, and without oxygen the brain dents and collapses as easily as crushing an empty Coca-Cola can. Five minutes?

She led me to my father's bed, partitioned off by curtains in a large area with other patients spread throughout. The nurse returned to a station guarded by plate glass windows. My father's eyes were halfway open, lids sliced across white-blue irises, lids that nurses slathered with Vaseline to keep them from drying out because he no longer blinked of his own accord. Prone. Chest lifting and falling only as the oxygen machine dictated. White gown opened at the sides. Tubes. Bags of liquid. The paleness of his eyes startled me, like the shine of tin just under the water's surface. He was there, my father, and he wasn't.

I had difficulty picturing the specific color of his eyes—a pale blue, not like the sky or the miles of shallow sea between sand and coral reefs, but a blue that whitened when angry. Was there gold flecked through? "Just flew in," I said, embarrassed talking to him this way, knowing he couldn't respond. I thought of the people surrounding us in their own beds, shadowy lumps spread out behind curtains. I patted his wrist and left my hand where his watch had always been, now a circular tan line. I felt the unmistakable meter of his pulse. Staring down at his unresponsive body, I, too, wanted to say the right thing that would wake him.

"I—" I was terrified. There was nothing about my immediate life to convey, because this was ground zero. We can build from here, I thought. Just wake up and we can build. I had made it in time, hadn't I? I'd gotten on a 6:00 a.m. flight, and I was here, I thought. And I would be here. When he woke up, I would be in this room or in the lobby. He would be drugged, dazed. Incognizant? *When* he woke—a vision of my mother feeding him baby food with a spoon flashed through my mind. A thin trail of Vaseline ran down on his cheek. I reached to wipe it off, and my finger came away tacky. I distinctly felt the scrape of his stubble and recalled how even when I was a teen, he'd wrestle me onto his lap and dig his roughened chin into the soft skin of my neck. I kissed my father's forehead. I hadn't kissed him since I was a very young child. My lips pressed against skin slick with sweat. It was a way of embodying him, this kiss. If I were lying in a hospital bed, that's what he would've done.

I hated the shared ward; his vacant, unblinking eyes covered in Vaseline; the curtains and symphonic beeping of machines; the squeak of rubber-soled shoes on waxed linoleum; and the stretchers already blanketed in white being carted around the room, the *earache-earache-earache* of wheels in need of greasing. This was not my father. My father was cool, strong, regularly dressed in faded blue jeans and pearl-button cowboy shirts, hair hanging down past his shoulders. He held himself like a hillbilly James Dean. Even the way he smoked, a cigarette clamped between his teeth or raised theatrically in the air, punctuating turns in whatever story he was telling—true ones, false ones, exaggerated ones—carried with it a cinematic charisma. He had a swagger that drew attention to his good looks, and he was handsome enough—six foot two with a thin, muscular body. In the summers, he cut his work shorts so high that half the pockets hung beneath the ragged hem. As teenagers, embarrassed by the amount of leg our father showed, Chris and I called him Daisy Duke. My father worked. He was responsible for making our little worlds run at full capacity without us ever having to notice. He was a provider. I often tried to imagine what kind of man he was when, at seventeen, he wooed my mom, a woman seven years his senior, a woman who lived with the near-disabling aftereffects of poliomyelitis. She had already been married. Kim was four years old. My father lived at home with his mother and stepfather in Paragould, Arkansas, working full time pumping gas at a filler station in Dyersburg. That's how they'd met. My mother worked as a delivery driver for Fox Photo and was often sent out to counties that surrounded Shelby, dropping off pictures to people who paid extra to avoid inner city Memphis. The first time, she'd stopped because her gas tank was low, but soon she found herself plotting, saving deliveries near Dyersburg for the end of her route. But she wasn't entirely sure about him. My father seemed so young, she says. He was hyper. Always bouncing from one thing to the next. When he talked, it was like chasing rabbits. I have a picture that my mother snapped while he filled her tank—"First met: September '74." He's dressed in an ash-gray company shirt, charcoal slacks, and a deep-blue jacket. The wind blows a lock across his face, angled shyly to the side, a smile, cautious perhaps, or just flirting. His head is too large for his body. He is growing into himself, becoming.

My dad's brother, Freddy, arrived on furlough with an armed escort the following morning. When Freddy took the elevator up to the public ward, the guard accompanied him. When my family smoked and talked outside, the guard stood silently behind us. Freddy was allowed to wear blue jeans and a beige work coat. He'd always been kept at a distance from my siblings and me. When my father was twelve, Freddy was arrested for robbing the local church, an event with prolonged repercussions, causing, first, the family to be barred from services and, second, my father's permanent distrust of organized religion. The grief and embarrassment his brother's actions had caused his mother were enough to make my father hate stealing, a distaste that hardened almost as much as his resentment for a preacher who spoke of forgiveness but offered none to his family. But it was not Freddy's absence throughout my childhood or the armed guard or the various convictions—meth, armed robbery—that made his presence so extraordinary. I was startled by how much he looked like my father, how his mannerisms and inflections were distinctly cast from the same DNA. The laugh, the way he stood with his shoulders squared, I saw these shared traits in Chris, sensed them in my own movements.

"What do you do?" he asked me during one of the few times we were alone together, smoking beyond the sliding glass doors.

How to explain who you are to a man who shares the nose and ears and, eerily enough, the same head cock and smile of your father? Even though he looked much older than early fifties, with mottled skin and white hair, his eyes moved with a wily jitter. As with most relatives I had spoken to since returning to Tennessee, this question proved difficult. A new, colder light would slide into their eyes when I shared my itinerant lifestyle. "I just moved from Washington State to Oakland, California. I'm enrolled in college. Community college. I've been touring with my band for the past four years, and I love it, playing music, but—"

He smiled. I saw in his expression that this news of his nephew (a kid he hadn't seen since Ninja Turtles were cool) both confused and interested him. "Why the hell you in California? It's a joke out there, man. A money suck."

"Tuition is cheaper in California than where I was living in Washington," I said. This wasn't the whole truth. I hadn't chosen to enroll at Laney College in Oakland because credit hours were less expensive than at community colleges in Olympia or Seattle. I'd chosen the Bay Area because if my plan worked, I'd be able to transfer to the University of California, Berkley, within two years, and the idea of earning a bachelor's degree in literature from a university with such tremendous clout seemed the only way I could erase dropping out of school. Grandiose plans were my greatest motivator.

"Must be schools near here. I talk to your dad some, you know. How's it hurting you to live closer?"

"Out there I've got to work harder for everything."

Amanda walked through the automatic doors just then, trailed by the boy who still lingered. She asked for a cigarette, and I gave her one. I hugged my little sister's shoulder. "You need sleep." Her eyes were black on black, and her teeth clattered.

"Smoke a joint and crash for a while," Freddy added. He then turned and walked inside, the guard following close behind. This would be the last time any of us saw him alive. He would soon die of liver failure in prison.

For the next two nights, I slept in the waiting room next to my mother at Jackson General. I did not find sleeping at the hospital all that bad. The fluorescent lighting, the crumpled way in which I laid across two chairs—my mother, upright with an afghan over her chest, next to me—and the weary cigarettes taken throughout the night wasn't unlike living out of the van on tour. Unsettling as it was, solace existed in those aching hours. Half-asleep in the brightness, I thought about trajectories. My father had built his home, my home, based on an inverted image of what he knew of his own father, a migrant farmer and alcoholic who left his family when my father was young. This propelled my father toward a working-class livelihood complete with cable and a car per parent, school clothes, and red meat. He was determined to provide a better life than what he had grown up with. Perhaps I'd inherited wanderlust from his father, Jo John. Or perhaps I, too, thought prosperity existed beyond the boundaries of home. Both my father and I discovered early on, after all, that adulthood could be different than what we were shown.

II

December 30, 2003. Dr. Jones summoned my family into a conference room. She was a young black woman with hair parted in the middle, and I'd never seen her before and wouldn't see her again. Her job was to interpret, and she held folders against her chest.

She said many things, and she said them with compassion. But all I heard was "The EEG reports show no brain activity. Hospital recommends removal of life support. In some cases, we would keep the patient alive, but the small cell cancer has metastasized. There is an overwhelming amount of sepsis. Even if the EEG had come back normal, the cancer is too advanced."

"What's that mean?" my mother said. "He has pneumonia."

"From the level of cancer cells in his body, I'd guess he's been fighting this since early fall. September or October."

My mother continued to argue against the report, to tell the young doctor about antibiotics Dad had been given for pneumonia, but each time she spoke, she lost her breath. She covered her mouth. Why would he claim to have pneumonia when he was fighting cancer? He wouldn't do that to us, I thought. He wouldn't lie. I tried to navigate my shock to a more realistic conclusion, one that my mother seemed to reach at the same time.

"I'm going to sue that goddamned doctor in Camden," she said. "You know when I told him about my pain, when I tried to tell him that I hurt all over, he didn't listen at all. He was smiling like an idiot, and I told him, 'Stop smiling that way.' You know what he said? He said, 'Ain't you a feisty one!' I knew we should've never gone back. And now this! It's his fault."

Dr. Jones opened a folder from the bottom of her stack and reviewed what was there. I asked her directly whether my father's file said pneumonia or cancer. I asked quietly, having walked away from the chaos encircling my mother—some tones accusatory, others consoling. The doctor seemed unnerved to find me so close. Her eyes would not meet mine, and she stuttered when she told me, "I'm af-fraid you're father's records are confidential, even from children." To the room, Dr. Jones raised her voice—"Please let the floor nurse know when you decide." She said *when*, not *if*.

My mother slept with my father that night. Even though it was against policy, she threw such a fit that she was allowed a chair beside him. By morning she understood the decision was now beyond her. And yet only she could sign the form authorizing the removal of life support; only she was responsible for the burden of making his death final. Few can rationalize the role my mother was forced to play, even when the act can easily be intellectualized, reasoned through, even though *brain* death medically constitutes *death* death, even when not a single organ in my father's body was free of disease. We all participated in that signing, but she was forced to hold the pen.

The door to my parents' trailer was unlocked, slightly ajar. I pushed it aside and stepped into near darkness, though it was midafternoon. Thick curtains blocked the sun. I was met by the smell of rot. I palmed along the inner wall, vaguely recalling a switch for the overhead light somewhere near the entrance. I hadn't noticed a glow from the computer, but now I saw Amanda hunched forward in a swivel chair, her eyes inches from the screen. She did not acknowledge Chris and me but continued clicking the mouse in steady time.

Chris reached below the couch, digging around for something.

"It's not under there," Amanda said.

"You can't take Dad's things," Chris said, and went into her room, just off the common area. He returned carrying a black tray with gold *fleurs dis lis* along the edge and a bouquet of prince roses in the center. Our father's rolling tray.

"Dad doesn't smoke anymore," Amanda said, still not looking up from the computer.

She was the reason we had driven eighty miles east to Birdsong. My mother wanted her at the hospital even though his—what to call it?—*procedure* wasn't until tomorrow. There was now an *appointment*—3:00 p.m., Sunday, December 31, 2003.

Chris dug a quarter ounce from his knapsack and began separating the buds from seeds and stems with Dad's little pair of scissors. Amanda's eyes were puffy and red from crying. She didn't say anything at first, just watched Chris break apart the buds until it was a fine shake. He then spread it evenly into the envelope he'd made of a rolling paper. He placed the entire joint into his mouth and pulled it out slowly, just barely wetting the paper before setting a flame to the whole thing, hardening the exterior. Stoner science.

The kitchen and living room were separated by a half wall and linoleum flooring that began where the carpet gave way. In the sink, there were pans and dirty dishes covered in pasta sauce and spaghetti, uneaten chunks of a sandwich. Roaches skittered over the plates. Stuffed in the corner near the table was a living pine tree, not the plastic foldable deal I'd grown up with. My mother had told me about it over the phone; everything was so crazy she'd said—"With Daddy down sick and no one else here besides, Amanda and I thought a real tree might brighten up our lives." Half the presents were unopened, with torn wrapping paper tossed around the table. I'd learned too late that they opened gifts at the table so that they could lift them up for my father to see from his place in bed down the hall. He was too weak to stand. Part way through Christmas morning he threw up blood. I'd been sick before, bad sick, feverish enough to have no concept of time, just the nodding in and out of balmy sleep, and so I understood this sort of weakness, the kind that erased days of your life. My father, no matter how sick, surely would have made an effort to stumble to his recliner and watch the youngest of his children open gifts. I knelt and picked up the wrapped box closest to me; it bore his name.

"Let me hit that," Amanda said.

Chris leaned back into the couch, and he sucked on the joint. Even for all his slobbering, the cherry burned one side irregularly. He dipped his finger between his lip and lower gum, pulled out a string of saliva, and dabbed it below the marred edge. Then he hit it again, without acknowledging Amanda's presence. It was a game they played, making believe the other didn't exist. Amanda watched Chris hit the joint a third time. The smoke was thick, drifting in blue ridges throughout the room, lifting slowly to the ceiling. Again, she asked for a drag. Chris just smiled, inhaled. In a flurry, she jolted from the chair, knocking it over. She clenched her fists and released a piercing howl. Everything about the way she moved, from her hunched shoulders and limp hair blanketing her face, was in this moment exactly as it had been when she was twelve, the last year that I'd lived with her at Meda. Chris, with his shithead smile, joyous now that he'd gained such an animallike rise, had lived with her off and on, up until recently.

"Smoke her out, man," I said.

"Alright, damn." Chris passed her the joint.

The lights were off, and my parents' room was steeped in further darkness by layers of curtains hung over the windows. I could barely make out the shapes of things. Carefully sliding my feet across the floor, I came to the edge of the bed. I groped at the mattress. The blankets were turned over, the sheets damp. My foot kicked something on the ground, a sudden clonk. I reached forward, clumsily grasping for the lamp. I found the switch and shocked the room with light. At my feet was a pot with congealed vomit moving gently at the bottom. There was dried blood on the pale sheets. This was *his* side of the bed, closest to the back door and the hallway entrance in case of an intruder. There was an imprint in the mattress, a bean-shaped divot. I couldn't shake the belief that, yes, he had known all along of the cancer and that he'd decided to cover up the severity of his illness so that—*Why?* No, he couldn't have known? There was no way anyone could weather such a large secret, let alone my father. He was too honest. But he was also private. Wasn't it true that he'd hid his panic attacks for a year? Could it be possible he wanted to hide his cancer as well? That he wanted to die at home instead of in a hospital. If anyone knew of his terminal disease, his last days would've surely been spent monitored. He'd had too much interaction with hospitals as of late. Had he thought there was more time, longer than a couple of months? The sickness advanced quickly. I saw the room, the vomit, the unmade bed—I heard the excitement in his voice when we'd talked about quitting cigarettes, when he said he admired me. I heard the doctor's summation that his cancer had been full-blown since early fall.

I cried, and with no one in the room to witness, my entire body quickly gave in to the pain in my chest. I'd never cried this way before, with my entire body, my mind electric with spasms of memory. Memories, loves, and regrets seemed to release from deep within, and I did not want to share. Remembering was the most private and dedicated way to interact with my father's dying. I reached to turn off the lamp and saw that his nightstand drawer was ajar. Next to a prescription bottle was the novel I'd written. I picked up the book and saw the inscription. There were dog-ears every few pages, as if he'd been studying.

III

In the hours before my father's death, we waited. We waited for the scheduled hour, without the luxury of speaking to him or of being understood. We waited still. Executioner and spectator, we waited. Sons and daughters, we waited. We breathed and walked and smoked and drank coffee out of cruelly small paper cups until a nurse came for us and said, "It's time."

There were only facts, like the sun glinting off a silver tray—pretty, blinding, harsh. My father was transferred from the open ward and into a suite. A room deemed private because it was not shared with others, not partitioned by curtains. My family stood like sentinels shyly fanned in a half circle away from the bed waiting a reprimand—*Hadn't we been on watch? Hadn't we watched closely enough?* I ingested the scene as if it were my duty to paint every detail across all synapses labeled FATHER. My hands clasped at the crotch of my jeans, hiding the little circle of piss, a consequence of rushing from the urinal too soon, rushing to meet my family when my mother's name was called over the loudspeaker. My brother hunched into his crossed arms, one niece, one nephew, and two sisters down from me on the other side of the hospital bed. My mother held the webbed apex of pointer and thumb so close to her teeth that I worried she might bite down. She swayed next to the bed, as if moving to a rhythm only her nervous system knew, a tune that played beneath her skin. The oxygen machine made its own music. *Pssshh-sumph—pssshh-sumph, beep-beep-beep.* Two nurses accompanied by two machines fidgeted next to his bed, scribbling, cautious to avoid a stray glance at my family. It was not an enviable job—flipping down the switch. And when one of the nurses politely arranged cables and tubes, straightening them out, setting each one away from my father's arms, my mother stepped forward, the first to move, the first to approach the bed, and grabbed on to his hand.

My mother gripped his shoulder and slowly, as if not to wake him—*Didn't he work early? Wasn't he overworked?*—and tried to crawl beside him. But the bed was too tall for her weakened legs. And so she hoisted, again, pulling on the sheet, on his torso in an attempt to get the rest of her body near.

"Don't, Mom," Chris said.

As if relieved to play an active part, the nurse asked, "Do you want to?"

My mother didn't answer, but instead, she rested her face in the pit of my father's arm, breathing heavily, one leg still caught up on the bed, the leg she had little control over, while the other held her weight by the toes. I was proud of her in this moment. Shouldn't we all have held him this way? Shouldn't we have smashed chairs against walls and broken out the glass windows; shouldn't we have torn our clothes and lit the retractable bed on fire, prayed, sang, at least reassured my father's spirit that he would find his way through death? I willed myself closer to the bed, but I could not force my body forward.

The nurse informed us of the time. Three o'clock. Kim helped my mother down. It was then that I noticed a roving beneath my father's eyelids. The nurse looked around the room, offering us one last moment of peace. When her gaze reached mine, she held eye contact briefly before turning away. Her hand moved quickly, and once she flipped the switch, the bright, green light shifted to clear, shadowed plastic.

My breath caught as my father's body lurched forward, his cancerous lungs choking my ears with his every failed capture of air. His eyes opened, but they did not search the room. I silently begged him not to search the room, not to see the family circling him, and I hoped the damage done to his brain had severed all ties to memory, to love, so that as he looked out from those wild eyes, he could not recognize any of us. But I had no way of knowing what he saw. My father's back arched and fell heavily against the bed. Then nothing. His blue eyes dulled but did not close.

The hospital provided us with a hospitality house so that we could all sleep under the same roof. It was a nice house with hardwood flooring, new appliances, and a claw-foot bathtub. *Wizard of Oz* played on the television. I bitterly watched Dorothy survive Oz and return home. Or rather, I felt the movie had played its audience false. Color or no color, Dorothy would've been changed by her experience, and she would never again access the same solace Kansas—home—had once provided. My mother lay with her head in Kim's lap, her feet across the knees of her grandchildren, Hunter and Hayley. She alternated between sobbing and total silence, her entire being both immediately present and absent. This distance in her stare scared me.

Neighbors set off fireworks, and flashes of purple and red lit up the picture window in the living room. It was New Year's Eve. Tomorrow would be 2004.

Chris called me outside, and we stepped into a paved four-car lot where his truck was parked next to Kim's Trans Am. There was a light dusting of snow over everything. Chris sat in the driver's seat, with the door open.

"You should stay for a while," Chris said. "You can always go back to school."

I was winded with the kind of breathless exhilaration that comes after a car crash or a fall. I lay down on the frozen asphalt. With stars and the moon in a clear sky above me, the smoke from my lungs mixed with the smoke from my cigarette while Chris talked about how we needed to protect Mom from herself. She might try it, he kept saying, but he would not use the word *suicide*. He was right, and I knew he was right. I didn't know how to express that we were on the same page. The longer I lay on the cold pavement, the less I knew what role I played in the world. Gone—a self too fragile to stick around, to depend on, and so, a hollow place.

"I feel like some essential part of me has just vanished."

"Don't say that," he said, kneeling. "I can't do this on my own."

"What are we supposed to do?"

"Dad always said—he told you, too—if anything happened, we were responsible for Mom. We're not putting her in a home."

"You don't have to be Dad," I said. "You don't have to be the only one."

"Who, then? You? I doubt you'll even come back. It's me. Just me. Kim's in Florida, and I can't trust you. The only person I care about right now is Mom, and if you're too selfish to do the right thing, well, that's on you."

What did it mean to leave California? It was only community college in a region I'd yet to claim. The South was covered in memory, like shadow. "It's a hard choice, man." I stood so that I could face him. "I agree with you. But I need to think."

"That's so like you," he said. "Just do whatever you want."

"I'm asking for some time."

He cut the ignition. "See you inside."

A single deafening BOOM followed a flower of purple sparks just on the other side of the house. Then came a second, brighter flower of white and another loud crack. I walked to the front porch so that I could see the display. I waited for a new explosion so that I could orient myself, or at least imagine what lay in the distance. No flash followed, and suddenly the calm residential street fell into the silence of below-freezing temperatures. So quiet that I could hear the trees creak and groan against the cold.

XII

Memento Mori Part Three

The Howlers

At the front of the school bus stood a boy of perhaps twelve. The door had been removed, and he hung dangerously close to the road, singing a throaty *¡Palenque, Palenque, Palenque!* He called for passengers, even though all I could see beyond the gaping hole where a window had once been was impossibly dense rain forest, broken on occasion by clusters of houses painted primarily blue and pink, towers of smoke rising from trash fires. I'd taken the cheapest transportation possible from San Cristobal, Chiapas, to Palenque. Because the bus leaving from San Cristobal had been delayed from its original evening time to five in the morning, I'd slept in a set of woods near the terminal. The following night, I had also slept, for similar reasons, sitting upright with my back to the station wall. When I woke, vendors had already begun setting up blue-and-orange tarpaulins over stalls. Sunlight filtered through the colors, making the cobbled road look like stained glass. I bought a new pair of socks from a man who had insisted on selling me Hilfiger—*¡Te gusta! ¡Te gusta!* In response, I had pointed to my torn jeans as if this somehow demonstrated the vast difference between Hilfiger and me. To the vendor, hearing only my John Wayne pronunciation—*No me gusta Hilfiger*—I had been *norteamericano* and therefore must love Tommy H. "Mire," he said. "¡Estados Unidos!"

The bus hit a large pothole, bouncing woozily on piss-poor shocks, and my mother's wedding ring slipped past my first knuckle. I'd lost weight, and the ring no longer fit my pinky as snugly as it had when she'd given it to me before I'd left for Mexico.

That night, she called me over to where she sat at the kitchen table. I hadn't noticed the envelope until she patted it gently, lovingly. A year was too soon after my father's death to face anything surprising. When I asked her a second time what was inside, she impatiently held out the envelope, and the ring dropped heavily to one corner.

"This was the second ring your father gave me. We were broke when we got married, so our first ones were turquoise. The seventies, y'know?" She smiled. They hadn't had the money then either, but he had worked odd jobs to scrounge up enough for the new rings. My mother had been pregnant with me; Chris had been a toddler; and Kim, a teenager.

"You can't wear it. Keep it someplace safe."

I thought of the T-shirt I'd stolen from his dresser the day of the funeral. I kept it sealed in a ziplock bag so that it might contain his smell. I would often take the shirt out and bury my face in the armpit, bringing his bodily presence into the room. The ring, like his shirt, had become a relic that I looked over and touched and wore and sometimes put in my mouth, letting the cool metal clink against my molars. His premonition that I would *burn out* if I did not choose stability over travel, choose steady employment over art, seemed dangerously close to fruition. I sometimes longed to sacrifice my ambition, to wash myself clean of error, but it was too late for me to change. I thought of this often—my desire to reconcile individuality with my father's notion of loyalty, my inner dialogue, a hybrid of our voices. I was distrustful of my intuition. I came to Mexico, as opposed to staying in Tennessee or California, to understand my exile, self-imposed or otherwise, as a fatherless son.

The bus slowed to pick up a European couple followed closely by a man carrying two wooden crates full of hens. The woman asked the boy, in Spanish, about fare while her partner, agitated, clumsily removed his large pack, shucking it from his shoulders so that it fell sideways and toppled the hen crates to the ground. Two chickens escaped. The chicken man was skilled, however, and quickly caught the hens by their feet. He sat across the aisle from me, cages at his side, feathers and dust raised by the wind, and I saw something beyond anger or embarrassment in his expression, a naked exhaustion perhaps. He reminded me of my mother.

Because I'd temporarily misplaced my passport and then my mother had forgotten how to find the airport, I arrived with less than an hour before my international flight boarded. By the time we pulled into the area for departures, she was so wound up she did not move her driving leg in time (she needed to grab beneath the knee to physically place her foot on the brake). The van careened through the drop-off zone, and we hit the high curb at considerable speed before she'd found the pedal. The van came to a jarring stop. My mother hid her face against the steering wheel, breathing heavily. This was how we said goodbye, an intense and clamorous farewell. I hated leaving her, shaken, parked half on a curb where it was illegal to remain idle.

"Will you be all right driving home?"

"Just go, honey," she said. "Don't miss your flight."

A week passed before she replied to my worried emails, telling me she had pulled to the shoulder and waited nearly an hour before her breathing calmed. I could've kept better track of my passport. I could've driven, of course, or at least kept my cool and not barked at her when she'd missed the turn for the airport. My mother's physical and mental acuity had declined since the funeral. Her body had been diminished by grief. She'd lost so much weight that the skin around her eyes and mouth sagged. At night, she talked to the pillows, spread lengthwise down his side of the bed.

If my presence at home could have helped, I'd come too late. My mother had convinced me to stay in California, mailing a check for three hundred dollars. The money had come with a note: "Use this to buy books, honey. Daddy and I are proud of you." I allowed myself to feel heartened by the plural pride of my parents, my mother forming a thread between the living and the dead.

I visited her on spring break my first semester. She picked me up from the airport wearing the same work coat of my father's that she had refused to take off all those terrible days at Jackson General. I expected a grief-stricken weekend, and I was surprised by the way she hugged me and chatted before I could stow my bags in the van. She ignored my pleas for rest and insisted we eat dinner at a Chinese restaurant in Camden and then go grocery shopping. She wanted me to teach her how to cook for one person. Her meals had grown inconsistent, primarily apples and crackers. For thirty years she'd slept with my father, depended on his consistency: home around six every evening, in bed at nine, falling asleep at eleven while he watched television. They had grown up together. He was seventeen when they met, and she, twenty-five. Now, at fifty-six, she woke alone. Made coffee alone. Smoked alone. Busied herself by rearranging furniture or painting various rooms in her new home.

When we arrived at the Chinese restaurant, the proprietor called her by name: Mrs. Linda. He gave us a free order of egg rolls after she'd introduced me as her son. "I come here too much. He's sweet, isn't he? Always says hello." Later, at the grocery store, she talked to the checkout ladies and the manager, and they shook my hand when introduced. She was mobile and clearly free from the anxiety that had affected my father, and therefore her life, for years. She'd been a good caretaker, a responsible partner, but as we scanned the grocery aisles, stocking up on smaller quantities for smaller meals, her demeanor seemed surprisingly open. She assumed that back in California I, too, was soaking up the world. "You go on living, because your daddy can't," she'd said during one of her late-night calls. I hated that it was the opposite, that I found my father's panic expanding within me. I wandered the city, without expectation, uninvolved with my surroundings. *My father's dead.* I repeated this while riding my bike from Pill Hill to downtown for class and then to Albany, where I worked at a pizza pub. I would think *My father's dead* and flash on brief but bright memories, sometimes full of smell, sometimes flooding my mind with loud sounds.

After the grocery store, my mother turned down Sunset Drive, and all the lightness between us vanished. Before the old trailer came into view, my eyes sharpened. A long patch of young growth rolled by outside my window, darker forms on darker forms, and then, seemingly hacked out of the forest was the half acre my father had cleared. The single-wide was lit up with music and voices as Amanda and her friends partied. In my mind, only half-opened presents, a real tree, a pot with vomit, and blood dried on the sheets existed inside that house.

Just beyond what was now my sister's home was the new double-wide. My mother reversed her van into the driveway, close enough so that the hatch nearly brushed the siding. We didn't talk, guilty for the banter we'd previously enjoyed. Here was where she grieved, as one prays in a church. Only out in the world was she allowed reprieve from supplication.

My mother made her way up to the front door as I grabbed groceries, and when I turned around, I saw she had no front steps to enter the house. Two rows of cinder blocks were stacked one on top of the other. She had no railing for balance, and the blocks only reached two feet off the ground, just tall enough for her to reach the knob. I watched, speechless, as she stepped achingly to the first set and reached her arms to length, opening the door. She used the knob to pull herself up to the next set of blocks, just high enough so that she could unlock the house. She had to shimmy the rest of the way inside by crawling on her stomach. Hundreds of clips from documentaries about poverty and loneliness and aging and disability shot through my mind all at once. I'd never witnessed a scene as devastating as this, and it was happening to my mother. She wanted me to see that she could do it, to see she was capable of entering and exiting her house even without stairs. As a polio survivor—as a woman who had come of age in and out of institutions—loss of independence frightened her most. Taking armloads of bags to the threshold, I lifted them up for her to grab, realizing then just how far the entrance was from the ground.

I spent the rest of the night in bed next to her, in the place where my father would have slept. After so much uncertainty about my mother, it was nice to simply watch television, waiting for her to doze. It was uncanny how much her bedroom looked the way my parent's room at Meda always had: the bed centered below double windows covered in layers of curtains, the television set on top of the dresser, floral pillows that matched a floral bedspread. The two nightstands were the same; as were the lamps. This was the first time I'd ever laid where he normally had. My mother lay next to me, her feet swollen like puffer fish and propped on pillows. She fought sleep, often jolting awake and then turning to me, apologizing, offering the remote. I kissed her goodnight and went to the kitchen to make tea. While the water reached a boil, I heard talking and peaked around the corner. She'd drawn pillows down the length of her body. Her back was to me: "He's doing real good at school."

The bus passed through Palenque's *zocalo*. Dust kicked up in great torrents, and the smell of garbage and *carnitas* wafted through glassless windows. I was starving. I sat up, alert to my surroundings, until the bus idled at an intersection and let the Europeans and me off at a rutted gravel road. The hostel I'd chosen promised hammock rentals beneath *palapas* for three U.S. dollars a night. Locker fees were also three bucks, so six total. Pennies mattered.

I stored my bags in a locker and walked to a small taqueria I'd noticed from the bus window back toward town. It was dusk. The landscape was extraordinary—along the horizon, variations of orange and purple with thousands of fireflies flashing yellow. To my left, the jungle stood like a fortress wall, dense with nothing observable beyond the front line; an enormous fig tree's roots like legs in the geological act of walking arched and intertwined, breaking the ground beneath their steps.

There were no other customers at the cantina, and I sat in a plastic chair close to the owner, an elderly man who shuffled toward me in chewed up loafers, never lifting his feet from the dirt floor. I ordered veggie tacos and a Pacifico. The proprietor flipped a switch, and rows of large colored bulbs flickered to life. The beer, when it was brought, was hot. I downed the bottle in three long drinks and asked for a cold one when he came with my tacos. He laughed and told me his refrigerator was busted, said he'd sell me beers half price because they were warm. I asked after sangria instead, washing down my tacos with the sugary wine. I'd brought a book, *Oryx and Crake,* which a man named Thomas had insisted on giving me the night before I left the small river town where we'd met.

Thomas was a quiet, serious man of nineteen who taught English at the language school where I was practicing Spanish. He wore the same khaki shorts and loose linen button-up every day. His white-blond hair was always cleanly combed, parted to one side. In the coincidental ways things happen, Thomas was on the bus nearly every time I went to a theater far outside town. Eventually, he invited himself to the movies with me—*The Aviator,* according to my journals. We spent the rest of the night discussing books, film, and travel. Mexico was his first time away from home.

"It's difficult," he said. "Mum and Da have been everywhere, even the Congo. They pushed me to come here."

When he said this, I recoiled. Thomas must've noticed a change in my attitude. Without a word, he pulled the hem of his shorts up toward his hips and revealed wide, pink scars that covered his upper thighs. Huge swaths of muscle and fat had been cut away. "A lawnmower," he said. "At my house there's a hill out front, and one day, I tripped." He'd lost a critical amount of blood. There was talk of amputation. His body brightened with transfusions. Surgeons switched to talking about skin grafts and tissue regeneration. Thomas finished high school in bed, and when he had healed enough to walk again, the skin still incredibly sensitive to open air, to the soft touch of fabric, he did not have the drive to do much. "For half a year I sat at home and read books."

The night before I left, Thomas's parents came to visit. We ate dinner at a high-end restaurant on the river. Waiters wore starched shirts, the tables had candles, and Bach's Cello Suites played over loudspeakers. Out across the river, I could see night fires from the rural part of town where there was no electrical grid for the poorest citizens.

Thomas introduced me to his parents, and when I sat down across from them, his mother poured a glass of Riesling for each of us. His father was perhaps fifty, and he looked his years, with deep creases around his eyes and a face gone flat with time. She was handsome, with thin wrists and exceptionally long fingers. I admired how her smile contrasted with her ruddy, sunburned skin. They were both doctors, Thomas had told me beforehand.

"We do a lot of work for Doctors without Borders. Thomas calls it activism, but truthfully, we love travel," his Mum said. "I love travel, I should say. Henry loves languages and adoration."

At this Henry laughed. His face reddened from his wife's teasing.

"What is it that you do?"

"He's a writer," Thomas said.

I felt as if he had shared a secret of mine for his own gain, and I was embarrassed.

"I'm not," I said. "Not really." Immediately, I was overwhelmed by a pressing need to tell them I was not a writer but a man who'd lost his father. I repressed this desire and made a conscious decision to keep his death to myself. It was a practice in owning my grief. After a time, this confession had begun to feel like blame. I pretended to be a normal person traveling alone, and to some degree, however briefly, it helped.

"He's written a novel and is drafting a second one. Don't fool yourself, mate," he said to me. "Whether you're good remains to be seen, of course."

"What is this novel about?"

I had been working for hours at a stretch expanding a short story I'd drafted just before my father's death. It was about a man who fled from home as a child, but now, deep into the future, after he'd nearly outlived his traumas, he was forced to confront his past unexpectedly. "It's about exile," I said.

As long as we drank and talked, Henry ordered more bottles of wine. I was fascinated by how easily I was able to talk politics—the insurgency in Iraq was in full swing—and how swiftly we could change topics from war to art. These people valued their son and, by extension, seemed genuinely interested in how my mind worked, not my body, and this, even though it was everything I'd wanted from adults throughout my life, felt like a betrayal of my father's memory. He would've distrusted these people, and they most likely would not have respected him.

Later that night, Thomas walked me back to my room. We made a plan to meet the following day and take a bus to San Cristobal. I left without him.

I found a cheap motel where I stashed my things and went out in search of mescal.

The next afternoon, I walked to Iglesia Guadalupe, a small temple known for its endless steps and view of the square. I'd only eaten granola and ran out of water almost as soon as I left the hotel. By the time I made it there, dehydrated and hung over, I was winded. Halfway up the stairs, I lay down and dozed off.

"You just fell out there?" It was Thomas, staring down at me. I don't know why I assumed he wouldn't make the trip. "No note? I waited, you know."

I shook my head; standing up, the sick mixture of beer and mescal swayed in my stomach. "I'm sorry. I needed to leave."

He nodded. There was nothing to say. "You look like hell."

Thomas coaxed me up the stairs, saying things like, "just a little farther," which made me angry, and so I'd say, "I'm taking it slow." The view, for all the steps, was less than brilliant. The church was ordinary. He and I laughed at this: all our efforts, alcohol sweating out of me, all in the name of beauty, in the name of experience, had brought us here, to this common church and simple view.

I awoke before dawn, dry mouthed and stiff from a night swaying in my hammock above the dirt. I showered and walked to the Mayan ruins of Palenque. I had expected intimacy, a private moment to stand within this demarcation of not just history but of cultural extinction. I was experiencing something no one else in my family had ever encountered; my expectation of the moment was to feel expansive. And yet the scene did not feel life altering; nothing of humanity's long, violent, and beautiful continuum was revealed. It was a lovely national park, well maintained with landscaped green spaces and cordoned ancient structures. I photographed the ruins—*A snake and skull engraving—good—and now Temple of Inscriptions.* I ate lunch on a grassy knoll that overlooked the jungle. I shuffled down paths, at times brusquely passing slower couples, slower families, slower tours or keeping pace with the dumbfounded many. Besides the ruins, there was a waterfall and the jungle and howlers grunting in the trees; a colorful snake slithered in front of my boot as I walked down stone steps that curved into the forest where I noticed a shrine among tree roots. There was a stone pool and a faded engraving. I imagined the shrine, concave and tall, as a fountain for ablution before sacrifice. If this place contained human sorrow, these woods seemed to no longer recall. A park employee appeared from farther down the path and cranked up a leaf blower. He wore large red earphones and clear protective glasses and waved to me as he directed the machine at the gravel path, smoking without interest.

Outside the gates, I took a trail where the guidebook mentioned ruins to which "an adventurous" backpacker could trek free. The jungle interior was hot and muggy, and I was quickly covered in sweat. Mosquitoes clung to my shirt and jeans. The guidebook did not say how far the ruins were from the main gate, but I walked long enough to grow concerned. When I spotted a small structure fifty feet or so off the path, open on all sides with stairs leading to a platform, I pushed through the underbrush and climbed the steps. It reeked of piss beneath the crumbling overhang, and in one corner there were liquor bottles.

A little farther past the ruin, I saw the silver reflection of water. As I walked through the jungle, burdened by my daypack and camera, I had no visual measure beyond shanks of sunlight until the canopy thinned near a pond. When I stopped moving, mosquitoes flocked to my arms and neck, covering my clothes, and I ran to the pool, stripping, tossing each article into my bag.

I covered my body in freezing handfuls, eventually sitting, immersed no higher than my hips. I crawled across stones and into a narrow, dark pool the width of a car tire, and when I knelt, the water rose to my chest. I dunked my head under and listened to my blood, a throbbing at the base of my skull, and then released, coming up for air, my skin taut with cold. I wiped my eyes.

It was then I heard the deep and terrifying growls of howlers. They were not very large monkeys, but their call was fierce. I'd never heard more than a couple at a time. For a moment, I even closed my eyes, listening and wondering what they were communicating, until more joined in and the howls grew frantic. I feared an approaching predator and slowly left the pool, keeping all directions in sight. The howlers were deafening now, and I stumbled to my bags, throwing on my shirt and then my pants. The monkeys followed, and the canopy swayed. The noise intensified. My only thought was to get back to the trail, but they followed me there too. The howlers leapt limb to limb, shaking the branches, and their calls turned to screams, horrible screams. And I realized that I was the threat. I was surrounded. The screams strengthened so that there was a chorus of *grunt-grunt-grunt* and *screeeeeeee-screeeeeee-screeeech*. I had yet to see one monkey, and as I walked up the trail, trying very hard to keep from running, I whispered to myself, "Please don't come down." I expected them to descend on me at any moment, their tiny hands tearing at my clothes and skin. I thought I might die this way, alone on a muggy jungle trail, trotting clumsily with my pants undone, shoes untied. Inexplicably, I began to laugh. The monkeys howled, and a violent wave of laughter erupted as genuine, childish joy. My father *was* dead. My mother was alive, perhaps cooking a single quesadilla and considering maroon paint for the kitchen walls. But I was almost twenty-four, I thought, and very much alive. Chris was too, hands blackened with grease, maybe eating a burger, occasionally hitting a joint saved in the ashtray. And Amanda, awake for days, speed keeping her company more than dreams; Kim and Hunter and Hayley, at home in Florida, perhaps moving through work and school, learning the language of adolescence and middle age. I laughed. And then suddenly, as if I'd crossed some invisible threshold, the monkeys stopped chasing me. I ran fast now, tossing aside branches and bramble. I heard the howlers calling at my back, but with distance the sound grew less threatening. Their cries quieted. *I'll be okay*, I thought. *I'm okay*. I stopped running altogether, alone again, grateful to be on this side of the chase.

XIII   Rain over Memphis

I don't hear the stairs creak until my father is almost to the foyer. I'm in his house, unannounced, sitting naked on a ladder-back chair. The television is on with the sound muted. I've been fighting scabies for eight months, and this is my third attempt to rid myself of the welts and itchy patches caused by microscopic parasites. My skin is covered in a thick layer of ointment called Lindane. I wait for the chemical to turn from milk white to translucent; I wait until it files deep into my skin. Lindane has to cover the body for an eight-hour period without being disturbed, which is why I am naked in my parents' house, awake at 6:00 a.m.

My father looks at me with tired, overworked eyes. "What the hell are you doing?"

He isn't angry. He is wary.

I tell him the rash I have is scabies. I don't tell him the whole bit about why I'm naked. He trusts me. His underwear has holes in the front and back. "You should ask mom to buy you some new tighty-whities," I tell him. "The skid marks reach around from both sides."

He laughs. It isn't a laugh, laugh. It's more of an "aha" or an "uh-huh." It means "funny." It means "smart-ass." It means "good job." "Love you too."

He coughs. Pushes his hand through his long hair. Shakes a cigarette from his pack of Cambridges. Lights it. His hair drifts back down over his eyes and sticks to his trimmed beard.

He asks if I want any coffee, and I tell him yes.

I hear him in the kitchen. A thump of tin set hard on the counter, a rush of water into the filler tank, and a clap as the lid closes. He goes into the bathroom and shuts the door, screech of rusted hinges.

I turn the channel to weather. He would have anyway. He likes to watch, without sound, over coffee, and in the early light. The coffee maker bubbles. I listen for him to come out of the bathroom. The Weather Channel shows footage of a flood. A hot spell in the far north has melted glaciers. For a moment, before going back to the safe and anonymous graph, it shows people in canoes floating next to pitched roofs. I am glad he missed this live footage.

I doze. I don't hear him come in with the coffee, but I wake when he sets the cup down on the cherrywood table he made for my mother. The table he lost his thumb building. After the saw severed his thumb, Smokey, our gray cat, caught the top half and ran out of the house. My dad grabbed a towel for the gushing blood and chased after her. His brother, Freddy, fainted. My mother screamed and shook in the hallway. He didn't catch Smokey, and she never returned home. I watch now as he puts another cigarette to his lips with the half thumb and pointer finger, lights it, and leans back in his recliner.

My father coughs and the smoke billows out. I am eager to be in this moment, few as they are, few as they have ever been—a moment for just the two of us. We haven't talked much since I moved out two years before, at sixteen.

"How much longer you got to sit like that?" he asks.

"Two more hours."

"Could you move then? I wasn't a glassmaker. You ain't

see-through." He gestures to the television. His smile. Cigarette buckled in his teeth. Steam of coffee. I stand up, embarrassed of my testicles, and move the chair.

"What's there to see?" I motion to the green-and-blue map on the screen. A red graph snakes down from Ohio, alongside the Mississippi River. Rain over Memphis.

Through the living room window, the sun spreads low in the morning light, humidity rising faster than the temperature. I imagine the Mississippi pulsing beneath the Memphis bridge, alongside the Tennessee and Arkansas border, and on down to the Gulf of Mexico.

"Dry as a bone ain't it?" my father asks, cigarette held between his forefinger and the hard dual mound of bone raised from his half thumb.

"Looks like a sunny day," I say. But I know it'll change. The light will exist long enough to cast shadows. Those shadows will vanish under the water-weighted clouds.

"It'll rain," he says.

"I know," I say.

I will wake up sometime later, and my coffee will be cold on the cherrywood table. I will lie on the couch, covered by an old quilt. Without a discernable memory, I will know he wrapped me in the blanket and moved me from the ladder-back chair. Somewhere in the house, my mom will be vacuuming. The gray light will creep in through the window, and the sun will sit barricaded behind storm clouds and thick rain. I will get up and go to the bathroom and bathe. Out there, in the city somewhere, my father will be driving in his truck or standing in an empty house half-remodeled, and he will smile when it starts to rain.

XIV   Ornamental Stairs

Mom had traveled away from Birdsong to visit Kim and my nephew
and niece in Sarasota, Florida, taking Amanda with her as a driving
companion.

Chris and I brought out Dad's tools from the shed and placed
them on a tarp to avoid dirt and moisture. As we set up sawhorses,
slashed and mended by our father's hand, as we locked new bits into
his drills, as we read over his residential carpentry book to figure
out how to turn a two by twelve into a zigzag of ascending steps,
I felt the true work was in this invitation to sorrow and memory:
the keening of the saw blade, the inhale of sawdust, and eventually the sour reek of our sweat mixed with our labor. Though our
task was to build a set of stairs leading up eight feet to the back of
our mother's trailer, the construction was purely symbolic. Mom
had difficulty with the four steps that led to the front deck we had
built the previous summer, and so it was impossible to imagine the
effort it might take for her to leave through this high exit. But she
ultimately would and stubbornly often, descending on her bum
one step at a time to plant and then water tiger lilies and primrose.

Chris drank coffee with a cigarette between pointer and middle finger. The steam and smoke rose around his face in the cool morning. He carried himself as the man he was, a nine-to-five mechanic with a girlfriend and stepdaughter—the laborer stance, an odd blend of punchy and sedate. This is to say that Chris seemed chipper even though he moved slowly. That year, living in Asheville, I worked manual labor too, but on my own terms, avoiding salaried positions so that I could prioritize touring with one of my two bands. Now, I tired easily, yawning and pinching my nose. There was no question of who was in charge of the construction; I did not have a mind for schematics and dimensions. Chris, on the other hand, loved the puzzling and stood for nearly an hour drawing and redrawing flat lines along the wood, worrying over the exactitude, because if an eighth-inch difference in the rise of a stair could trip us, then how might Mom fair?

We did not talk much. We hadn't in years, really, but frequency in conversations had plunged since Dad's death. Today was no different. We both tried, I think: How's your job? *Fine.* How's your band? *Fine.* I wonder now if this reticence didn't originate from mutual fear (or knowledge) that we simply did not care about the things that interested the other. Siblings, after all, are spitefully honest with their feelings.

"Hand me the T square," Chris said.

I did.

He smoked an entire cigarette before he marked the measurement.

I asked to take over.

"Nah, man. I don't want any mistakes."

"We'll be here all day."

I saw that he meant to defend his moves, but he quickly smiled and tossed me the T square. I found the angles in the residential carpentry book and marked the step, purposefully speeding through the actions, all to prove a point. Chris checked the work and found a failed angle that would have made the stair lean inward at the rear. I shut up after that and sat down on the tarp with my coffee.

With only one step measured and marked, he pulled a tin can from the bag of tools he'd brought. There were four or five rolled joints inside; he lit up. I felt a familiar sadness. Soon after this Chris's eyes would shift, and he would become impenetrable to me—a sloughed smile. But the joke was always inside the high, and I think this was where his love of weed derived, as though he welcomed this splitting in two so that a part of him could move inward to a safer place. I knew that this—being with your high while with others—was part of the social expectation. I drank alcohol in a similar fashion.

"Take a hit," Chris said through a clenched throat.

I didn't want to be separated from my brother as the sober one, but I said no. "I can't smoke, man. It makes me crazy."

What I feared would happen did. The light around Chris changed, dampened a little, and soon a part of him was obscured.

"I'm going to deal with the cats. I'll come back to help after you've measured."

"They'll be fine," he said.

"Yeah, but I won't. The fleas are eating me alive."

"You'll come back?"

"I'm just here," I said, pointing to the house.

When we'd arrived, Mom had been gone for three days, and she'd left the air off. The trailer was humid as a greenhouse. Fleas had bred happily in the heat and covered my ankles and shins when I walked through the door. Her indoor cat had gotten out and come back home just before Mom and Amanda drove away. My cat, Miette, was staying with Mom, because at the time, I lived in an illegal shack in a set of woods behind a soccer field near downtown Asheville. No one in my family knew this. I was happy there, but some things are best kept from family. In the shack, I had a kerosene stove and lamps, a bed and couch, and a three-hundred-gallon rain catch; it was no place for an indoor cat. Miette was a calico with a long tail, and we'd traveled together for eight years even though I'd never intended on calling her mine. What happened was this: She'd been dropped off at the first house I'd ever rented. I kept my distance, ignoring her, but one night, I woke up to go piss and found that I couldn't move my head. I had long hair, dreadlocks, and I reached back and discovered she'd made a nest out of dreads on the soft pillow. I still did not name her, but afterward I let her sleep in my room. Then, she'd gotten pregnant, not yet a year old (she was spayed directly after), and I kept her inside so that the kittens would be safe when the time came. A month later, I woke up in deep summer and felt slime and weight between my legs. I pulled back the sheet and saw that Miette, though she still didn't have a name, had birthed three kittens on my crotch. She came to me, afraid but purring, and soon went into labor again. I traveled with Miette out west—to Olympia and Oakland and back south—but not to Asheville, because I did not plan on staying in that small town. Years later she would die at seventeen in Iowa City, but in regards to this memory, she was only nine and so covered in fleas that they visibly crawled across the white of her fur.

Mom had flea bombs and flea soap in the pantry. I grabbed a beer and took a swig from the Knob Creek that Chris had left on the counter. It was before noon, but Chris was stoned and he was not going to let me help build the stairs. I moved the litter box, food, and water into Chris's truck. Mom's cat struggled and fought, pawing my arms though she had no claws, as I shampooed her beneath the warm water. Her coat was marbled and brown; the fleas collected in the draining pool. After drying her with a towel, I put her in the truck. There was plenty of shade, and the fall afternoon was only warm in the sun. Miette did not struggle. She sat patiently, staring up at me. The fleas swarmed her face, the one place where I was hesitant to shampoo; they collected in her eyes and around her mouth. I ducked her head under the faucet and swiped them away. The water blackened.

"I put the cats in your truck," I told Chris. I'd set off the bombs and carried in my arms a couple of beers and a glass of his high-end whiskey.

"Why? Just leave them inside."

This horrified me; they would die, of course, if I left them with the chemicals.

"You're joking, right?"

"I left my cat inside when we bombed, and she was fine. Just lock them in a room where there's no carpet."

"Oh," I said.

"You thought I meant just leave them out? Like I'd do that."

"I didn't," I said, though I had thought this is what he'd meant. "The poison could still slip under the door."

"I stuffed a towel—are you drinking this early, man?"

"You just lit a joint."

"It's different."

And it was. I knew this; Chris smoked hourly. Stoned was his normal disposition, while being sober or drunk for him created an altered state. For me to get drunk meant an immediate but short-lived inebriation that could get in the way of building the stairs. "I'll go easy," I said.

By the time we had measured and cut the braces, the allotted three hours for the bombs had passed, and I opened the windows and doors, grabbing a fresh beer and snort of Knob Creek. Chris had lit another joint and was smoking by himself, drinking a can of Dr Pepper and leaning against a tree a few feet away from the tools. I veered toward drunk. I don't recall what I rambled on about, but I was not paying attention to what I was doing when I picked up an eight-foot-long two-by-twelve board and walked it over to the sawhorses. The back end of the board hit the side of the house in such a way that the edge nearest my body suddenly grounded and became a barricade and rammed my stomach. I was knocked onto my ass. It did not hurt or wind me but simply shook up my natural movement. I'd been loosely carrying a board, unanchored, and then suddenly, it was a stiff brunt. Chris laughed, spitting Dr Pepper into his cupped hands, the joint dropping from his fingers onto his lap. I laughed as he brushed the cherry away while still trying to save the joint from falling to the grass. We were loosened; the laughter settled my nerves. And I felt lighter, until I didn't, until I could not stop the laughter. Chris could not stop either. His face turned red, and a vein in his forehead throbbed. We fought for breath. And then we stopped, as if our breathing was tied by the same threads.

"You're such an idiot," he said.

I mimicked his surprised expression and the silly way he fought to save the joint and staunch the burning pants. This started a fresh bout of laughter from us both, a simpler exhale that did not feel as violent as before, and I realized that I'd been taking short breaths from the top of my lungs the entire day and that my body now seemed to luxuriate in long inhales until my torso loosened and I finally relaxed. Chris seemed to do the same.

The last time we had been alone together was the day of our father's funeral, and we'd begun a fight that had not been reconciled.

With Dad's life insurance, we had bought the double-wide that Chris and I were now building steps for, leaving the old single-wide for Amanda to live in for a time.

The night of the funeral, the trailer was full of relatives and friends. There was standing room only, and people talked loudly, ate leftovers with their hands. My mother sat smoking at the kitchen table, responding to occasional remarks. When she caught my eye, I mouthed, *Are you okay?* She waved me over.

"Where's Daddy's picture?"

She was referring to a photo in a silver frame that she'd brought to Dad's wake. Before Chris and I carried his casket to the hearse with the other pallbearers, she came to me, holding the picture, and asked that it go with him. The director was nowhere to be found, but the preacher stood at the head of the procession, waiting to lead us out. I took the photo to him. The preacher raised my father's cupped hands and placed them over the frame. He then closed the lid of the casket.

"With him," I said. "Buried."

"Why?" her voice cracked. She set her teeth. "What's he gonna do with that photo? It was mine! Mine! Mine!" Three times—each repetition growing in volume.

I stepped outside and opened the van door where I'd earlier hidden two tallboys. Chris followed. He put his hand on my shoulder and told me not to sweat it.

"I'm cool," I said.

Chris passed me a hip flask of Southern Comfort. "What's your plan?"

My plane ticket back to California was set for the day after, and spring term at Laney College, where I was enrolled, started in a week. I'd felt certain this would no longer be my trajectory. Not then, anyway. I'd supposed I would move into Mom's new home and then, after things had settled down, return to Memphis. That's what I told Chris.

Chris shook his head, his eyes alive with something close to fury. "Nuh-uh. Only Mom is gonna live in her new house."

"If that's how you feel, then I'll move to Memphis. I can actually get a job there anyway. Buy a car. Or borrow one of your cars."

"No," he said. "You need to watch after Mom until I move up."

"You don't get to choose where I live. Have you talked to Mom about this?"

"I don't have to," he said.

Fierce, regressive anger welled up inside me, and I punched Chris in the arm three times, as hard as I could. He watched me and waited for the fit to end, as was his way, as he'd always done when we were children.

In the backyard, next to the half-built steps, I was about to ask Chris if he'd thought about that fight recently, because I'd all but forgotten, feeling instead as if our current relationship was a collection of unresolved fights and not, perhaps, simply rooted in this one. But he was thinking of something else, another time that also took place on the same land and in front of the single-wide trailer where Amanda now lived. This was before anyone *lived* on the land at all but simply visited regularly.

"Look at this, man." Chris held up his thumb and showed me a thick scar that ran the length of his thumbnail. "Remember when you shot me?"

We were barely adults then and had traveled to Birdsong for the weekend. After swimming in the river that first afternoon, as I was walking up the steps and into the trailer, Chris procured a BB rifle from somewhere and promptly shot me in the ass at close range. I chased him, weeping, and eventually wrestled the gun away. I raised the rifle and aimed. He was breathless with laughter, looking exactly as he did when I knocked myself down carrying the board. He picked up a small plastic bucket, yellow with a white handle, and pretended to shield himself. I fired. The BB went through the bucket and lodged into the skin of his thumb—"Damn it! Look what you did." His voice was high and whiney, and he sniffled and wiped his nose. But he did not cry.

It was near dark by the time we'd cut and screwed down the steps. While Chris tacked up pickets along the railing, I vacuumed and wiped down the house. The stairs looked nice, and with the project completed, Chris grew talkative, giddy with accomplishment. We ate frozen pizzas and then crashed on Mom's bed, flipping through cable with drinks on our respective nightstands, ashtrays resting on our chests.

A music video aired on MTV. I didn't recognize the band, but the production was the same overly sexualized shots of women dancing that have been a staple of music videos since the beginning. This one was of the pop-goth variety—an all-male band playing in a dark warehouse surrounded by long legs and barley concealed cleavage. One of the women had auburn hair and freckles, and she made me especially uncomfortable, because she looked very much like the last woman I had dated, a difficult affair that had left me raw.

We'd met one month after Dad's death. She lived north of Oakland in Napa and contended with bipolar tendencies sans medication, and I fought grief and clung to her without an understanding of what living with an unmedicated bipolar disorder actually meant.

"Damn, man," Chris said. "What I'd give to hook up with any one of those girls."

"That one, the redhead, looks like my ex."

Chris made *psht* sounds and shook his head. He stood up and all but stomped out of the bedroom and into the kitchen. I wasn't sure what had set him off but could guess he thought I was being arrogant. I heard him open the bottle of Knob Creek. I still had a full glass, but an empty beer, and so I asked him to bring me one from the fridge. He did. He set it next to me on the nightstand to telegraph that he wasn't full-blown angry, just annoyed.

"Why do you always do that? I get it, man. You're the pretty one, and girls like you. But do you have to throw it my face?"

"Your girlfriend is pretty."

"That's not the point—like, our whole lives, you've been trying to best me, when you know I don't have a chance." To make his point, Chris popped out his entire top row of teeth. He wore dentures at twenty-seven. His teeth had begun rotting at twenty.

"Don't throw a pity party, man. I can name every one of your girlfriends, and all were attractive and lasted longer than a year. I've never had a relationship go more than nine months."

"It's because you're such a fucking gigolo, is that it?"

"No. I just haven't fallen in love. What's better: fucking or companionship?"

"Who's throwing the pity party now? *Poor little baby has to hook up with all the pretty girls!* Remember Lynette May?"

He pulled this name from the archives, so far back in our young lives that I was shocked to suddenly remember that there had once been a Lynette May, and yet I recalled her vividly.

Chris and I had met Lynette and her friend Hope at East End Skating Rink during one of the many Heavy Metal Nights we attended. Lynette was tall and fifteen, like Chris, and had long brown hair that hung limp over her face. She also had large breasts and wore short shorts. Hope was small and meek and had a blonde bob and braces. Chris, like Hope, was shy and chose to remain silent as opposed to flirt. Lynette, like me, enjoyed banter, and soon she began calling the house. She asked for me but always found a way to get Chris on the phone. I think Lynette's con set me off, knowing that she was using me to get to Chris. I was eleven. Puberty had hit early and hard. Lynette had been the first girl I'd talked to when sex had been all that I thought about. I started calling Lynette when Chris was not around, and our conversations quickly turned so pornographic that when my father overheard my end of a conversation, he sat me down for my first always-wear-a-raincoat conversation. Once when I was talking to Lynette, Chris quietly picked up another line and listened. After this, he refused to speak with Lynette, and he wanted me to do the same. But instead, I went out to Lynette's house.

I should have known something was off when Lynnette asked if Chris was going to come over too, but I had been too geared up on fantasy to understand nuance. Mom dropped me off at the apartment complex in East Memphis. I had condoms that I'd picked up at a craft fair in my neighborhood from an AIDS awareness booth. Lynette met me at the front door wearing makeup. Hers were the first breasts I'd touched, and she was the first person I'd seen in panties and nothing else. But suddenly, after an hour of making out, she stopped, pushed me to the side of the bed, and turned on the TV.

"My mom will be home soon," she said. *Tiny Toons* blared from a thirteen-inch screen.

My face must've betrayed my shock, because she laughed and said, "You didn't *really* think I'd fuck you? Oh my god, you did!"

She stomped out of the room, laughing a fake laugh with no cinema at all, and returned wearing Umbros and a faded Memphis Chicks T-shirt. "Don't sit on my bed," she said. I picked up a stuffed cheetah. "Don't touch that—don't talk."

To wash away my hurt, I lied to Chris and said that we'd gone all the way. Lynette's name was never mentioned again, and eventually she stopped calling. It was not something I thought about much after the residual impact, and Chris never brought up his involvement with Lynette, until now.

"I really liked her, man. And you went behind my back."

I'd never thought about it in such simple terms. I knew that Lynette had used me to get to Chris, but he'd never said anything about liking her and had kept all his interactions with her secret. He was right, in a sense. I had gunned for her affection the moment I realized she didn't care for me, but by doing this, I'd also betrayed my brother.

"Was that the first time you really hated me?"

Chris rolled his eyes. He was drunk and stoned, and that combination reversed his typically stoic demeanor and could turn him weepy. He lit a cigarette and leaned back into Mom's pillows. "I didn't say that."

"You didn't have to," I said. "I lied, you know, about sleeping with Lynette."

"I know," he said. "She told me."

He said it was about trust, about me always being arrogant and self-involved. He said he couldn't look at her after she'd told him about me in her room. Another music video came on, of what I don't remember, and Chris said, "Stop talking. I like this band."

We fell asleep side by side on Mom's bed. I woke sometime in the night and found that we both lay near the center; his forehead rested in the small of my back. The room smelled of smoke and liquor, and I had a hard time falling back asleep. There were other beds in other rooms that didn't feel so swampy and smell of booze and smoke. But I didn't want to get up, and so I stayed next to my brother until the sun slanted through a thin crack in the curtains.

X V   On Love

1.

After living together for nearly a decade, Mesha and I held a com-
mitment ceremony in North Carolina. It was small, outdoors, with
our close friends and family. During the exchanging of vows, the
sky let loose and drenched us all.

We wrote our vows separately, and in hers she quoted Roland
Barthes: "When discussing the expression of phrases such as 'I
love,' he said that the lover who repeats these words must be like
the mythological Argonauts, who traveled with Jason to seek the
Golden Fleece and, over the course of their journey, had to replace
each part of their ship, so that they ended with an entirely new
ship, without having to alter its name or its form."

My vows declared love to be a verb; love must translate into action
always preempted by choice. "I choose to love you daily," I said.

2.

When I was younger, I thought of "falling" as the singular act of
love, as one might fall into the sea or muck. What happened next
depended on the ambiguous design of fate or destiny. Expectations

were displaced to the same outside forces that push people together in the first place. If daily interactions grew tenuous, ill defined, one could always spice the relationship with petty squabbles, hoping to free love from uncertainty once anger had passed.

3.

I fell in love for the first time when I was nineteen after a brief tryst with a person who had chosen the name Q. When we met, I was in the process of packing up my life in Memphis before moving to Olympia, Washington. We grew entangled within the coming separation. The combined acts of leaving and desire were cinematic. I watched myself fall in love as if I were a viewer in an auditorium.

In Olympia, after the first time I called Q from a payphone, I talked to her nightly outside a bodega. Date nights. I wasn't supposed to call. We'd made a deal. Letters were fine, but to hear each other's voices would invite heartache. While we talked of our past and questioned our future, we were quick to say *I love you.* We decided she should move to the West Coast. I had not found a job yet, but with the last of my money, I bought a Greyhound ticket; lied to Q, saying that I'd found a temporary job at a weekend fair; and showed up at her house in Memphis four days later.

Falling is a verb dependent on the continuous gerund form. This was all we knew of one another, immediacy, but when it came time to live within routine, we found ourselves incompatible. We tried, I think, to stoke the fires by picking fights; for my part, I redirected earlier passions into fantastic jealousies. In truth, my tantrums were a way of transferring responsibility onto Q. I did not want to believe that love could be replaced so quickly without an equally cinematic occurrence. Within a few months of living together, we separated, but neither could afford to move out. I hung a sheet between us in the basement room that we rented and slept on a couch. Nightly, Q drank wine and listened to Nick Cave and drew pictures until she was drunk enough to plead with me to come to bed.

4.

In bell hooks's radical book on love, she writes, "In our society we make much of love and say little about fear. Yet we are all terribly afraid most of the time." Fear, she writes, teaches us that security "lies always with sameness," so that "difference, of any kind, will appear as a threat. When we choose to love we choose to move against fear—against alienation and separation. The choice to love is a choice to connect—to find ourselves in the other."

5.

I was raised to believe in the pure mythology of love at first sight, based on my parents' three-month tryst before a tiny wedding in the living room of my mother's family home. What she loved was love, her love for my father. My father was only seventeen when they met, and he died at forty-eight knowing that he'd remained faithful and provided for her and his children. Is this not a reality turned myth, a clan first drawn together by love and then sustained by survival?

6.

When Mesha and I first talked, I worked in a video store. We knew each other from volunteering at a radical newspaper in Asheville. I was a copy editor, and she delivered the paper in a Radio Flyer wagon around town. She came to the store with a group of friends who searched the porn section for BDSM; she stood alone by the animated children's films. It was her twenty-second birthday, and she'd just gone through a nasty breakup. She wanted to watch something that might remind her of safety and home. The others, she knew, would never go for *An American Tale*, and when I said, "I've been wanting to rewatch that movie. It was my favorite as a kid," I was not hitting on her. Nor did I think proposing to watch a kid's film was a catchy pickup line, and so she surprised me when she asked for my number.

We did not have sex for months after we began dating. Within our promiscuous culture, this equaled a long period. She had only dated women before, and we were slow to build toward this frame of intimacy. My father had recently died, and with this loss, I no longer trusted people to handle my psychology gently. Before his death, however, I'd also convinced myself that I was an untrustworthy caretaker of others' emotions.

7.

I am unkind for drawing parallels between failed loves, because in the end, Q is not to blame and should not be used here as a proxy. It's just that I learned from Q, from our quick and passionate affair, that to fall for someone else is a noble risk.

After our relationship ended, when Q left the basement in early April, bound for a concierge job in Amsterdam, years passed before I could love another. I had sex sometimes, and occasionally, I spent longer periods with wonderful people. But I could not love. Few witness the daily self-abuses the thwarted lover undergoes. Everything Q said during those months before she left was true. I lied when I told her that I loved her, though I did not know I was lying at the time. I was incapable of letting another love me. But the most frequent accusation was this: "You don't even like me."

How easy falling in love was when we were both moved, or rather, moving?

8.

This morning, while reading over coffee, I was struck by a passage from Don DeLillo's *The Names*: "We must be more precise in the details of our responses. This is how we let people know we understand the seriousness and dignity of their feelings. . . . We must be equal to the largeness of things." I've cut one line that orients this quote within the landscape of the book, Athens, and I've disregarded the context because, more so, I read this as a definition for the terrifying position that love invites. To see love as a verb automatically means trusting another with vulnerable truths and accepting their trust in return.

9.

When I think of our first years together, trying now to remember what it was like to be afraid of love, I see us in Mesha's station wagon, at 5:00 a.m. on New Year's Eve. We were dressed up, smelling of cigarette smoke and cheap bourbon, and because this day of celebration always circles around my father's death, I lingered on sadness. I called my mother's cell phone. She had not, and still has not, changed the greeting that is simply his voice, bored and impatient, saying, "Linda and Chris." My mother answered that New Year, and I asked her to hang up so that Mesha could hear his voice. Mesha wanted to hear my father's voice.

10.

To say love is a choice does not mean I choose in spite of some glaring flaw; to choose means that I daily witness and listen and acknowledge love. Were I to ease into a state of forgetfulness, of expectation, I fear that love would become inactive as our shared epidermis and dust settled on the piano I no longer play. Falling, in the context of choice, is an inadequate form of movement. Love is a graceful suspension in a room with no gravity, the artifacts of life and coupling afloat in subtle play.

11.

In *An Alchemy of the Mind* Diane Ackerman writes that over time the chromosomes of longtime lovers "modify the brain, altering the self whose continuity we cherish. We don't just get under each other's skin, we absorb people."

12.

I remember, in 2012, after a year of frugality, I gifted myself diving lessons in Honduras. During the day, while I moved underwater, Mesha read and wrote on the terrace of the hotel that the diving school provided. In the evening, we met for dinner at one of the seaside restaurants. Sixty feet below the surface, swimming above brightly colored coral, the light diffused by distance and no longer blue but white as the sand below, I lost sight of the rest of my crew. For a moment, I panicked, stopping short of ascending. A flounder kicked free of the sand and silked into a whitish-yellow color; a sea cucumber, dark green, roused beneath coral pipes that looked like cartoonish megaphones. It was as if the creatures felt my anxiety. Before an instructor found me and guided me back to the group, what I thought was this: I am under the sea, alive beyond gravitational boundaries, and I am loved by someone who is perhaps at this moment wading in the pool or studying the character arc of Denis Johnson's *Angels*.

13.

"My world is a safer, securer place because of you." When I reached this line of my vows, I sobbed. I knew the ceremony would be emotional, but I could not stop the jag. To love, you must be responsible simultaneously for the other's feelings as well your own. This trust is based not on sexual monogamy but in the sharing of your psychology with another. I cried in this moment because I realized it was true—I did feel safe.

XVI   Dear Brother

Your girlfriend gave Mom a plastic pencil box that held a few of your belongings—a belt buckle, a Zippo, two cassettes, string fragments, a glass one hitter, and a photo of you—but I opened it only recently, having carried it around in an egg crate full of letters and photos that I would never consider tossing. Mom had driven down to Memphis from her new home in Birdsong, two hours, for your stepdaughter's birthday. She wanted to watch her open gifts, but your girlfriend did not let Mom inside. And so the child tore into the wrapping paper in the passenger seat. Your suspicions about another man, though you did not know his face or name, were confirmed when Mom was told later by a mutual friend that he had moved into your house.

I don't remember being in this photo, the one she sent. I only remember you. There I am, in the shadows. The memory is otherwise familiar. It's your thirteenth birthday. You're wearing your favorite shirt, a purple one with Rude Dog on the front, and these sunglasses with green—what are those things called? You know, the pieces that go from the lens to ear . . . We had matching pairs gifted from some fast-food restaurant. We never ate out, but I remember the day we got those glasses. A billboard advertised Wendy's in Mississippi, and I realized other cities besides Memphis had these same restaurants. You called me stupid for not already knowing this, because we'd eaten at Burger King in Arkansas the summer before, when we visited Dad's parents. It's funny how much you loved cars—a big Cadillac—but you never wanted to travel. You tried once. I nearly forgot. You drove across the country with your dog. It didn't go well, I remember. You were robbed in Utah. When staying with a friend in Seattle, her housemates mocked your southern accent.

In the photo, you're holding a red Fender that Dad got you, and a Crate practice amp is in the background. It must have been before Dad remodeled and Mom put up wallpaper, because the dining room walls are rose colored. Dad got each of us something big when we turned thirteen, and you got this guitar. Years later, in the warehouse you rented across from the Lorraine Motel, where Martin Luther King Jr. was assassinated, somebody robbed your place and stole, among other things, this guitar. You cried, I remember. You told me not to tell Dad. That warehouse was wild. No heat. No furniture. You didn't even own a refrigerator, and you swept the trash into the center of the floor. Once, you threw an all-night dance party, and fights broke out. You tried to break one up and got jumped. I can't remember how many individual brawls happened that night, like some story from the Wild West, and I didn't see you get punched. I must have been trying to make out with Lauren Coldwell. I always tried to make out with Lauren, a Mexican girl with green eyes and a ripped-up Crass T-shirt.

At your wake, they passed a different picture around. Someone wrote "The Crew" in the border. You are sitting on the roof of the Cadillac you bought from your weed dealer. It had a gold grill, gold rims, and wood grain on the inside. One morning, you woke up to go to work, and the car sat on blocks with the grill gone, the rims gone, even the gold hood ornament. In "The Crew" photo,

I'm standing below you with seven others. We're all making the three-letter sign CYC with our fingers, like gangsters. CYC—our neighborhood. Cooper Young Crew. The picture was taken at Barrister's, that back-alley club downtown. It must have been '98—I think His Hero Is Gone played that night. You are shirtless. You were always shirtless. You'd just gotten "Bugg Life" tattooed on your stomach like Tupac had "Thug Life" on his—later you added a backdrop with a barn and a haystack and a rusted-out Rambler. Bugg. Everyone called you that at your funeral. I wished you had a better nickname than *Bugg in the Ear*, all because you wore a spider earring in high school. Our friends who stood in the backyard at your wake had the same postures as in the photo. They were older. We all were. You were twenty-nine when you died. Does that mean you'll always be twenty-nine? I had moved away, and not many others had ever left Memphis. They wanted everything to be the same. They wanted to re-create "The Crew" picture around your casket. I refused. I didn't go inside until the time came to carry you to the hearse. That would have pissed you off, I know. I knew then too, but no matter how many times I tried to cross the threshold into your living room, I always turned back. It was because I wanted to talk to you alone but was never given the chance.

I carried you the way we carried our father. Our nephew, Hunter, walked behind me, and a few times he stepped on my heels. "Sorry," he'd say. "That's okay," I'd say. He was fifteen and strong enough to be your pallbearer. It made him happy. Even though it didn't. He rode in the limousine with the rest of your friends. "Stay with me," he said. But he protected me, in the end, holding my elbow while I shuddered next to him in the back seat, as if his slight weight might steady me.

I had visited you only a few weeks before, the first time in a couple of years. I brought my wife, Mesha, and because of your recent colon surgery, we made you brown rice and salmon. You hated the food, but you played nicer than your girlfriend and her daughter, who tossed the fish in the trash and ate bologna sandwiches instead. It felt nice, being with you, as though we were entering adulthood together.

Do you remember our phone conversation just before your colon surgery? Dad's death, the deterioration of his body, affected you more, because your job as a mechanic and smoking habit—both weed and Doral menthols—were so similar to his. You told me that if something happened to you, I should throw a party at your wake, none of that sad shit. I agreed, but when the time came, I tried to talk your girlfriend out of it, unable to imagine joy now that it was true. During that conversation, I told you I was scheduled to get a vasectomy the same week of your surgery. I asked you not to tell anyone else, because I knew that it would hurt Mom. You told her anyway. When I learned of this, I cared more about not getting a chance to share stories, like that there was a poster hanging from the ceiling above where I lay—a squirrel holding acorns with a caption that read, "Guard Your Nuts!" It's a detail I know you would have loved, guaranteed to make you snicker, but I could've knocked you out with laughter had I told you that after leaving the exam room, doped on pain meds, I'd misheard the nurse, a honey-colored man with gold rings. He handed me a plastic cup, and I thought he said to bring back fifteen samples. So over the course of a couple of weeks, I filled the cup with fifteen ejaculations and then brought it to the nursing station—*Is that what I think it is?* the nurse said. *What the hell am I supposed to do with all this?* It hurt to cum, hurt anytime I touched my swollen balls. Embarrassed, wanting the artifact to disappear immediately, I threw it away in a residential trash can. I can see you now, even though ten years has passed since your heart failed in the middle of the night; I can see your face turn red and the vein grow wide in your forehead; I can see your shoulders hunch forward and your light-blue eyes water. I love your laugh.

Ear stems! That's what the piece is called. You are wearing sunglasses with neon-green ear stems. Our hair looks ridiculous. Mine's a bowl cut. Yours is a mullet. Kentucky waterfall. Missouri compromise. It *was* 1991, after all, and no aspiring metal head would have had any other haircut. Thirteen—the age when ambiguity between soft and heavy metal is defined. One had to choose. Never did a Metallica fan cross over into Mr. Big. Soon after your thirteenth birthday, I ditched Bryan Adams and watched as you slipped into the realm of junior high and heavy metal. Did you notice me hidden in the dark edges of the photo? The younger brother. You were thirteen once and I was ten. I've been three years on your heels since birth. Just like in this photo. I remember the time I hid on the roof when I was six because I got my nose busted in a fight and I didn't want Dad to see that I had lost. You let me lean on your chest until I stopped crying. Blood on my shirt and yours too. You raced a train once and cut it off; once, you drove fifty-five miles an hour in reverse down Peabody. With the train, I held my breath and decided that I'd rather die with you. But while in reverse, we were older, and I screamed for you to stop and let me out. You were angry, and I walked the rest of the way home. I didn't trust you. Probably the first time, and this hurt you deeply. You were still the older brother, after all. Just like on your thirteenth birthday. Just like in this photo.

I miss joking the most. There was little room for humor after Dad's death. You felt the need to take his place, and I'd forgotten why leaving home had felt so necessary. I only knew how to navigate life through movement. I don't run so much anymore, Chris. I finished my undergraduate degree at thirty and went straight to graduate school. I teach now, and I write. If our family were still whole, I know you would've resented the success—first person in the extended or immediate family to earn a university degree— but not because of pride; simply, as the younger brother, it broke the rules we'd established about firsts. You were the first to find strong love. You were the first to buy a house, to build a career, to raise a child. You were the first to mature, and you were the first to stay home when Dad was ill. You were the first to drive to Birdsong and fix Mom's water pump, her busted pipes, and her roof. You were my first true friend. Thankfully, you were not the first to die.

Can I tell you something else? We built a studio on a piece of land in southern West Virginia, Mesha and I; we insulated the structure, hung drywall, put down southern yellow pine flooring, and built bookshelves and a bar counter that separates the main room from a little kitchenette. The work, Chris, I loved the work. When I sit down to write every day, I think of you. I think of Dad. I want to see you pull up in a Cadillac, reeking of weed, with grease staining your fingernails. I want to see Dad laugh as he rakes his hair back from his forehead. I accept it now, the absence, but the depths of these losses—the anger, perhaps—is also why I never opened the red pencil box your girlfriend gave Mom on your stepdaughter's birthday, until now. I remember it from our childhood, because you'd painted the center black one summer before school started, back when it actually held pencils and markers instead of weed and after that, I assume, where you tossed random things you didn't want to lose but had no immediate use for, like a belt buckle, a Zippo, a glass one hitter, and a photo from your thirteenth birthday.

XVII

How to Walk as a Nontraditional Graduate

Do not remove your front teeth, even though the plastic top cuts into your gums and even though the plastic tooth is too wide for the hollow spot. This will only draw further attention to your age, to the difference between you and the vast majority that surround you, skin smelling freshly laundered and teeth naturally white and healthy.

When you make mimosas before the ceremony begins, put them into breathable containers, perhaps cups with straws or sippy lids. Otherwise, as your sweetheart illustrates when she opens her stainless steel water bottle, the carbonated pressure that has built up will explode all over your gown and hair and up your nose and rest stickily on your eyelashes. Your sweetheart does not cry, as a traditional graduate might, because this absurdity blends beautifully with both of your participation in the ceremony. "When it rains, no one will know the difference," you say, and you both look to the dark clouds above. "Save my place while I go to the bathroom," she says.

When you feel the fidgetiness of a thirty-one-year-old who knows the internal rhythms of waiting—waiting at clinics, at the DMV, for work, for paychecks, for love, at hospitals and wakes, for grief to pass—when you feel this impatience building, remember: do not turn your irritation on those around you who seem extraterrestrial in all their effervescent joy as they shout and laugh and paint over the flowering magnolias with blue gowns, with yellow tassels, blue tassels, and yellow-and-blue tassels, the tassels being singular distinctions in this crowd, demarking those who simply passed from the summas and magnas.

Strike the impulse to downgrade your yellow tassel, to dismiss the work you put into earning your distinction as summa cum laude. Yes, you benefit from living a full decade longer than most surrounding you standing in this parking lot beyond the quad, and this might have allowed you an advantage over, say, the student who only recently left suburban America. Do not remind yourself that you feel as if you should not be here at this particular rite of passage, considering your previous trajectory.

Do not begin to ask yourself if this day came about because of the deaths of your father and brother.

Worry over your mother, who is bound to her wheelchair and the kindness of your sweetheart's parents, who push her to where she needs to go. Damn the doctors in her rural town for not issuing her an electric chair three years in a row now, even though she cannot walk more than a few steps at a time.

Know that she will not be able to live alone for much longer, but try not to think too far ahead. The time when she will move out of her own home and into your older sister's house in Florida is still one year away. For now, your mother can grocery shop on her own, as long as an electric cart is available.

Smile when recalling that your older sister and your nephew and niece were able to join you for the party the night before, but do not dwell on the fact that they had to leave early so that your twenty-one-year-old nephew could begin his tour as a soldier in Afghanistan.

Do not think about how you are moving, about your empty apartment, boxed and stored for the summer. The indoor yard sale and U-Haul bound for Iowa will come later.

When the temperature drops, text, "Here comes the rain," to your sweetheart, who sits among other Ms, while you are with fellow Os. And laugh when sheets arrive in torrents as soon as you press the send button. Join the others who scream and clap with acknowledgment of the unique spectacle. "This is the story of our graduation," you text before she has had a chance to respond.

When the rain does not stop, worry about illness; this is no time in your life to catch a cold.

"I'm freezing," she texts. "Will you come inside with me?"

Do not, for any reason whatsoever, leave your seat, even though the president of the university is still moving through her speech forty-five minutes later. She stands beneath a canopy and does not acknowledge the storm. In front of you, a row of graduation caps sink with water, and blue dye drips down the back of necks. Your arms, you notice, are now streaked with blue as well.

"Wouldn't it be funny if I peed myself in all this rain? No one would know." It's a silly thing to text, but an hour later, when the rain has not lessened, the faces around you pale with cold and blue with dye, while Erskine Bowles gives the commencement address, strongly consider the possibility.

For now, you think the rain will simply pass; afternoon showers are common in the mountains. Call your mom, and when she doesn't answer, call your sweetheart's mom. And when she doesn't answer, begin to worry if your mom is warm, if she is alone outside, if she is alone inside. Other fathers and mothers break the barrier to bring sons and daughters umbrellas bought from the student bookstore. Soon the view ahead—all those As and Es and, yes, even Ms, who will be called forth and find warmth first—resembles a hot-air balloon with the bulbous descent set to pause above the ground.

When your body recognizes equilibrium between outside wetness and physical immersion, the chill and discomfort subsides, and your body temperature regulates and feels not unlike swimming. Recall, as you always do when stuck in the rain, a night during the summer of your eighteenth year, the year you should have graduated high school, when, after a punk show, you drove to a gated community in Harbor Town with ten others and swam illegally in the large outdoor pool. This, as your senses engage with the memory, is one of your happiest. You all scream when the first bit of lightning strikes, and though you know the danger, you love the challenge. And you still do not know who kissed whom first, but soon you are all kissing one another, blindly trading mouths around and then splashing recklessly in the streaks of electricity. The joy of the moment was so pronounced then that you cried, and the rain hid this sudden burst of emotion.

"I found your mom. She refuses to go inside. A man gave her his umbrella."

When you call your mother's phone again, pretending paternal indignation, she answers. "This is the first time I've seen any of my kids graduate," she says. "Like hell, I'm going inside because of a little rain." Tell her you love her; always tell her you love her.

There will be a period when the waiting becomes too much and you are angry; those around you are angry. And one by one, each student begins to grumble to themselves and then to their neighbors, but when the recitation of names and distinctions creeps closer to your own, the shift in your relationship to time, to the wait, becomes magnanimous.

You are surprised that after you've been handed your actual diploma, the photographer still wants to photograph those before you. They are beneath a canopy, but you and those behind you are not. The leather encasement that holds your diploma bends with moisture even though it is covered beneath your robe. Smile. This is the only time you will be able to hold your diploma up for display without looking ridiculous.

Laugh when, after the photographer ushers you along, a volunteer takes your diploma and stuffs it into a large, black Hefty bag. The metaphor, though perhaps wrongfully bitter, makes an all-too-perfect joke on the fluidity and impermanence of knowledge and experience.

Now that you are with your mother, who is equally wet as you, who is shivering and wrapped in layers of coats, who cries and hugs your waist from where she sits in her wheelchair, and who won't let go so that you can see if your diploma is damaged, make sure to hug her back. Ignore the diploma for now. Because if you look, you will find that it is, in fact, crinkled and that a patina of yellow stains the center. Remember that you are someone who enjoys story and symbol and that this is only one moment within a much larger moment. Do not throw the diploma into the trash, and do not, whatever you do, respond to your mother's attempt to calm your fury by saying, "I don't fucking care about anything." Because this, shall we say, *tantrum* might bring you too close to the truth—that you are still a child of a mother no matter how old you are.

When you are home and you've changed into dry clothes, make a new mimosa to replace the original. Sit with your sweetheart in the empty kitchen and snack on cheese and crackers. Ignore the boxes and missing furniture. Laugh when you recall the events of the day. Be sure to congratulate her on finishing top of her class and don't brush it off when she says, "You really killed it, you know."

XVIII   Barking Hours

Fled is that music:—Do I wake or sleep?

JOHN KEATS, "Ode to a Nightingale"

Halfway through my mother's visit in mid-July, I decided to clean
the chimney. I raked a wire-bristle brush, attached to a pole more
than twenty feet in length, up and down the mortared shaft, filling the sky with dense and billowing soot. The smell of creosote
crept into my nostrils, and for the remainder of the day, I sneezed
black grime into a hanky. I did not fear fire, but instead, I remembered how, at Baptist Medical in Jacksonville, Florida, my mother
repeatedly yelled for the child only she could see to stop burning
sparklers, her face nearly hidden beneath a sheet. She covered her
cups with napkins. Bits of purple embers landing on her cheek
left a layer of grease, she said, and made her coffee taste like ash,
but what had to stop, what she couldn't take any longer, was that
damn creosote smell.

*

As my mother maneuvers her electric wheelchair closer to the
aluminum can she uses as an ashtray, coffee ripples along her cup
rim. Her eyes, just recently dull and drugged, are bright and the

color of lichen with gold flecked through. I see once again she knows the weight of things: the bone chill built by days of rain; the cautious look in my eyes that, at times, I sense she fears might turn to hate; her own cognizance and continence nearly lost to the slipping comfort of oxycodone. I watch her now, talking at me on my front porch in rural West Virginia, and it's hard to believe I once prayed for her death. Beginning with calls six months before, as she cried because she'd wet the bed or pissed on the kitchen floor a few feet shy of the toilet. Her movements are restricted by chronic pain; post–polio syndrome, her conjoined twin. But this immobility was something new, a brisk and confusing revision of previous abilities. "It's too cruel," she told me. "I don't want to live—this isn't a life." After this call, a circling wish, something keenly like need, had taken hold of me: *Please let her die before it gets any worse.* She's right—I told myself and my wife and my friends and my sisters—it's too cruel.

But she is here now, alert. Unlike before—What counts as before? One month? Two years, three?—when she could no longer read; when her words ran like a creek grown fat from rain, thoughts interjecting clause for clause; when she'd nod out midmovement, her hands miming the motions of quilting. She is like her old self now, and though I am reluctant to embrace such positive transformations, I love my mother and am grateful. Occasionally, I catch her eyeing me, a brief glance, an intake between storied memory. My mother's ability or, rather, trusting that others believe that she is capable is the bedrock of her worldview. I have been trained to believe that her strength exists beyond disability. In her forties, however, post–polio syndrome took root, and now, at sixty-eight, she can only manage ten or so steps at a time on her best days.

"Look, honey," she says. "There's a baby cow in your yard."

I see nothing across the summer green. Nothing hiding within clusters of locust and cherry and fencing that separates the neighboring Hereford pasture from my own land. No cow, no songbird, just the tawny hills and, farther beyond, the blue silhouette of

Flat Mountain. A tension settles between us. She smiles, shy but certain of what she has seen. I don't speak my fear, nor do I look back toward the pasture.

*

A flood ravaged the county where I live, the day she was found screaming, crawling on her elbows, dragging her useless legs down the driveway. In West Virginia the Greenbrier River submerged filling stations and storefronts and two-story homes, but it was the creeks that did most of the damage, swelling into one roaring deus ex machina. The hills, recently logged, were now without roots to soak up the rain. Because my land is high on the mountain, only the graveled lane gathered two feet of rushing water, and I drove my Toyota Yaris through this temporary creek—the undercarriage scraping over washed-out stone—in search of highways free of floodwaters so that I could be with my mother.

It had been raining in Florida too. Pools of water collected where the concrete driveway was split and cracked. But my mother saw sun. Her mind warmed, and she cried with fierce, unreserved joy now that she had finally broken free from the coffin her family had locked her inside for days without food or water—*They're killing me! Torturing me.* And suddenly an elephant led by a cigar-store Indian emerged from the light. She knew then, for a little while at least, she would be safe.

A neighbor called my sister Kim at work, where she manages sales for a blinds company. She's strong, my sister, willful. Without any outside help, Kim transformed a garage into the two-room apartment with kitchen and bathroom where my mother now lives. Kim had checked on Mom that morning, she recalls, before going to work, and found her deeply asleep on the floor next to the bed. I know this room well. Alleys of carpet crowded by antiques and half-finished quilting projects surround the large frame and mattress; layers of curtains darken the room. Kim tried to wake her, not wanting her to sleep all day.

"There's an ambulance and squad car outside," the neighbor said.

Minutes later my twenty-three-year-old niece also called: "Grandma's telling the cops we've tortured her, starved her. She thinks I'm hiding in a tree, shooting arrows."

When Kim pulled in front of the house, Mom recoiled: "Get away from me! Keep her away." Paramedics did not allow Kim to ride in the ambulance. Instead, she drove with her daughter and son, recently returned from Afghanistan, to the emergency room and waited. The delusions did not abate. "I hate you," Mom repeatedly told Kim. "I wish you were never born."

My mother saw feces on her clothes and hands: "You think this is funny? Bringing me here covered in shit?" She undressed, fighting her grandson off with such strength that he had no choice but to let her strip, hiding her naked body behind a raised sheet. A nurse brought a gown. She was kind to the nurses, asking if they had children, if they were married. My mother loves children, but more so she loves marriage. For eight hours they stood in a crowded hallway. Kim refused to cry when Mom retold this story of extreme abuse. And she told it often, pleading, fearing that no one believed her. If they did, then why was her daughter still here and not locked up?

Within twenty-four hours of her hospitalization, an MRI, CAT scan, and EEG were ordered. All tests came back normal. A neurologist visited, as did a psychologist, an internal medicine specialist, and two psychiatrists. None could accurately diagnose her delusions. Ultimately, her medications were named as a potential cause, and she was stripped of her thrice-daily dependents: Percocet (oxycodone and acetaminophen), atorvastatin, baclofen, cephalexin, fentanyl (patch), gabapentin, Keppra, levothyroxine, propranolol, ranitidine, Keflex. When my wife and I arrived the following evening, the imagined box and hunger and thirst and darkness that had closed around her were still very real. Over the coming hours, I witnessed her experience hallucinatory sound as voices in the walls; sight, a child with sparklers, purple embers; taste, ash in her drink; touch, soot greasing her cheeks; and smell, creosote. She had left home without her dentures. Her top lip sank inward. Diminutive, childlike, her head hooded beneath a sheet, she was elated to see my wife and me. She smiled and cried and retold the terrible story. We, in her mind, were coming to her rescue. Kim's pinched expression told me I could not expect forgiveness for this sibling transgression anytime soon.

I noticed a general hesitance from hospital psychiatrists to name opioids as the primary culprit for her delusions. I, too, was not certain her hallucinations had a solely synthetic origin. I named other malefactors instead: loneliness, grief, watching too much true-crime television, coffee. Her full-time companion is her own mind, after all, and I reasoned that no one could hold it together for long, being nearly bed bound with one voice primarily expressing a myriad of memories and emotions.

The first staff psychiatrist, Dr. Tran, argued that her pain medication should be restarted immediately. He suggested adding morphine to the list. As he saw it, she had a right to "quality" of life. This was his refrain. Dr. Tran had spoken with my mother during one of the rare moments when no family was around. Her hallucinations were still strong—she had been kept awake all night by partying nurses who were drunk and listening to rap music. She didn't know what the celebration was for, not yet, but it was wild. And soon she'd ask Gloria, she said, and Gloria would tell her.

Dr. Tran was the first doctor I had met since arriving, and I hoped this tall man with broad shoulders, wide forehead, and very small hands could translate the patterns of my mother's psychotic break. But he was grim, speaking firmly, interrupting all interjections and questions. Based on her pain levels, he said, and what was discussed during their private interview, he saw two options: let her live longer—"which is against her wishes as she's told me"—or manage her pain with higher doses of opiates so that she can live a shorter, yes, but more comfortable life. "Once a patient is dependent on drugs and the drugs cease helping sustain a healthy life, then the patient is, in essence, terminal," he said. "There are infrastructures put in place to help people who have *celebrity diseases*, like cancer. I believe the same attention should be given to other forms as well. Your mother lives with chronic pain that even the highest dosage of oxycodone cannot maintain. Now I ask you," he turned to my mother, "Do you choose quality of life or quantity? You can't have both, and the two cannot meet in the middle." Before leaving, he scheduled a counselor from palliative care to visit the following day. The two women brought my mother coloring books and markers for which she was very grateful.

My family reeled; so disturbing was Dr. Tran's certainty that an easeful death was the correct course. The nurses who had grown to love my mother were also troubled. In the hallway, I felt contemptuous glances from the island station. I feared they could smell my betrayal. Was Dr. Tran not voicing my own solution? Was I not, like Keats, "half in love with easeful death"?

The following day, however, a different shift psychiatrist arrived, and Dr. Tran's review was dismissed entirely. My mother remained on the full dosage of medication, because the new doctor believed that the hallucinations were caused by lack of restful sleep. Even though she sometimes slept for sixteen hours, occasionally whole days, he believed that none of her rest truly counted if she did not reach REM. For this, he suggested adding a new medication, one with proven results among patients who suffer from chronic pain.

Minimal research online reveals an indigestible amount of information about the sociological effects of opioid addictions and anecdotes of the people who live inside these facts: 80 percent of the world's pain pills are consumed in the United States; by 2013, detox clinics were dealing with suburban professionals such as lawyers, ministers, nurses, and cops, and opiate substance use disorder was named an epidemic; after federal restrictions on prescriptions were tightened and a new version of OxyContin was reformulated so that the pill could not be crushed for snorting or injection, the addicted turned to heroin; a sixty-milligram pill costs roughly sixty dollars on the street; the equivalent in heroin costs one-tenth of this price.

Of hallucinations caused by prescribed opiate usage, there are few responses from physicians or pharmaceutical companies. Generally, while reading lists of side effects, hallucinations show up in the double digits, just after fever, chills, and persistent sore throat and just before hearing loss. In 2003 Dr. Timothy A. Moore of Yale University wrote a letter to the editor of the *American Journal of Geriatric Psychiatry* concerning an eighty-year-old patient who complained of auditory hallucinations while taking oxycodone. For days, she heard "Ave Maria," "Silent Night," and "Jingle Bells" in their entirety, repeated continuously and always in the same order. "Each song," Moore writes, "was sung by a solo male voice accompanied by an orchestra." Her neurological exam was otherwise normal. I found a lot of forums where people sought community through their struggles. Some stories were desperate; some, resigned. Joe Graedon posted to *People's Pharmacy* in 2008, "My husband had hip replacement surgery in January. For two days after the surgery, he was a bit groggy. By the third [day] he was hallucinating. I was trying to prevent him from injuring his new hip while he was seeing bobcats, raccoons, cattle trucks and airplanes, all in the hospital room. He threatened to divorce me because I wouldn't take him home." In 2009, blogger Loolwa Khazzoom wrote, "I called my mother on Friday, expecting to light Hanukkah candles with her. She was crying and screaming hysterically about how, any minute now, the hospital staff was going to murder her. She wouldn't even let me get off the phone to call the nurse." In 2015 Daniel MacDuff wrote about his life post knee surgery. His marriage dissolved when the hallucinations began and he continued his dosage to counter the pain: "I can wear clothing over my legs without being in agony. I am able to maintain a family routine (as a single dad 50% of the time). Most people wouldn't be able to guess either that I was under the influence of heavy-duty opioids or that I was disabled. The time that is my own, when I am not needed to do the school run, or the days when I do not have custody, I usually give in to the hallucinations and let go of the pain and discomfort. There is finally a place where the pain can't get me, where I can sit down and enjoy a good conversation with friends, even if none of it is real."

My mother's hallucinations subsided by the time she was released. She was sent home, but she refused to sleep in her bedroom. In there, the nightmares persisted. Not just as remnants of hallucinations but with a tangible artifact: the box. She recalled her torture and dehydration and anger at the injustice of gifting trust to her daughter—it was too much, this waking dream. Nightmares she called them, not hallucinations or delusions or a psychotic episode. She did not allow anyone, not even doctors, to refer to her experience as anything but a nightmare. This addendum corrected questions about her sanity or ability; she was simply disoriented, living halfway between unconscious and conscious mental states. And so she moved a collapsible table and all her quilting supplies into the front room and slept under piled blankets on her couch. Here she stayed until, a week later, faceless men broke into her apartment and stole, among valuables, all her medication. The absent contours of the men's features were violently smooth, as if burned away. They moved so close to her that she could sense life within, smell creosote on their breath. She crawled once again beyond the threshold and screamed for help.

The staff psychiatrist at the new hospital, where she'd been driven after the faceless men, believed a buildup of opiates in her system caused the hallucinations. She is four feet ten inches tall and sixty-eight years old—the doctor observed—there is no way her body can maintain such high levels of opioids. He removed oxycodone and prescribed a lower dosage of hydrocodone. The hallucinations subsided, but a week later, one morning before leaving for work, Kim accidentally gave Mom an older pillbox that contained Oxy instead of the new prescription. Within hours, my mother had burrowed beneath blankets to keep from asphyxiating on smoke roused by children burning down her kitchen. Warm in her quilted cocoon, she dozed. She woke to Kim mowing the yard in the middle of the night. She screamed for her to stop, lifting herself into the motorized chair and wheeling outside. She beat the vinyl siding with her fist, but her daughter refused to cut the mower, the keel of the blade working its way into her mind, her ears alive with sound. She again crawled beneath the covers, and when she surfaced, she found the kitchen clean and saw that the grass was still high and thick. She recalled how her grandson had told her to look for evidence: *If the grass is high now—*

*

"Grandpa Arnold would sit out on his porch, just planks on the ground really, not a deck like this, and he'd take out his penknife and whittle little wooden foxes and cats. Never talked much, but when he'd finish one of those animals, he'd give it to me. He had the worst sense of humor, and when I'd walk in front of him sometimes, he'd take the crook of his cane and catch my ankle, tripping me. And he'd cackle!" She laughs at this, shakes her head as if she can't believe this dichotomy between love and cruelty was possible. He's been on her mind lately. All stories circle back to her grandparents' farm. Perhaps it is because she's visiting me on the mountain, or perhaps it's the realization that she is now the age of Grandpa Arnold and that she was once a girl who loved wooden animals.

I let her talk. She has been off oxycodone for two months and has regained mobility and mental acuity. And I believe she enjoys her memories more now that she knows they were nearly lost, and for this reason, she rarely stops speaking. Her stories continue even when I get up to refill my coffee. The porch is slick with rain. A fog from the valley moves through the Hereford pasture, obscuring the horizon and tamping shadows.

"Grandma Arnold cooked on a woodstove. Not like the heating stove you got but a big cast-iron thing with an oven and eyes. She'd stoke the burners and could set the oven just right with kindling and whatnot and bake birthday cakes. The house always smelled like creosote. You know? That tangy, bitter stink. I hate that damn—"

I watch her, always waiting for a relapse. The air echoes with her voice, her words billowing out until the last. She stares beyond.

"There's that baby cow," she says. I see fear in her eyes, a plea for validation.

And when I look, the calf is there, grazing halfway across the yard, male most likely, black with a white mask in the shape of a skull. A pair of my free-range chickens cluck at the ankles of the calf. The bovine eyes, glassy with pretty lashes, light up with worry before he runs, strangely fast for all his girth, up the lane.

"Stupid chickens," Mom says.

An adult cow, unnoticed until now, moos mournfully at the fence line, her thick lips pursed, as she calls after her yearling.

XIX   Into This Place

In my front yard, just beyond a cluster of grapevines held aloft by
a stick-framed arbor, is an outhouse built by the WPA in the 1930s
with the simultaneous goals of putting West Virginians to work
and, in a sense, modernizing the rural poor. My father-in-law is
the only one who uses the outhouse these days. In the late 1970s
he built a two-story home without power tools, because there was
no electricity, and his two daughters and son were raised walking
through the cold or dark across the lawn to the toilet. When he
visits Mesha and me from his new home in North Carolina, this
outhouse with pine hitch locks and open-air holes reveals such
a deep sense of place that by evening he is sometimes brought
to tears, not by sadness necessarily, but as a reaction to the ways
in which landscape carries memories, as if carved into the bark
and limestone.

The miners are here too—those who perhaps shat in this product
of FDR's works program and then walked down the mountainside,
whistling for one another in the predawn. The oldest family we
know of was named Highlander; the father was Minor, like the

melancholic key. Minor died and left his wife, Nellie, with children, and when her house accidentally burned, neighbors built a shack over one weekend with scrap lumber and spare windows. It had no foundation. There were gaps between the slats, where snow collected on the beds, and a milk cow came in at night, drawn to the heat of a cookstove. I eat meals off a table built by one of these men, a Phillips; he first carried the slats of felled cherry on his back down the mountain to the miller and then up again in planks ready for ninepennies and varnish.

For more than thirty years, the Highlander shack slowly disappeared beneath multiflora rose, blackberries, greenbrier vines, decay, and life, until all but one hinge was left for me to find when, this past spring, while clearing a fallen locust near the lane, I saw a cluster of red flowers. Out of curiosity I hacked my way through the thorny mess until I came upon a quince bush, which was once popular and does not grow wild. With a machete and chainsaw, I eventually rescued this ornamental shrub and intended to stop there, but then I saw lilacs in bloom through the bramble. I uncovered narcissus, lilies, honeysuckles, and a sassafras dwarfed by the weight of a fallen maple and now twisted with the effort of reaching for light. I do not know if it was the previous spring's late freeze or the large population of deer, but something shifted when March turned to April. And what once had been buried was suddenly revealed: Nellie Highlander's front yard.

I am an outsider here in West Virginia, a man who left Memphis nearly twenty years ago and has since lived in most regions of this country, and for this reason, I have often felt exiled from an understanding of home. I've carried the deaths of my father and brother as well as the love and trust of another, all without a place to return to. When I moved to this isolated piece of land, I meant to mend from grief, and what was unearthed for me as I worked to build a garden out of an old shack's front yard, etching blood and triumph into the soil, elated at each new discovery, was gratitude to feel a part of this place, to feel at home.

ACKNOWLEDGMENTS

I would like to acknowledge my sisters first. Kim and Amanda, I love you both very much.

My mother is a fierce and powerful woman who has supported me through the entire process of writing the essays that belong to this collection. Our memories often diverge, this is true, but she has always been willing to talk through our complicated and difficult story.

It would be an understatement to say that this book would not exist without the help of Mesha Maren. Mesha, you are my best friend, and I am grateful to enjoy this terrifying and beautiful life with you.

If I did not have such a deeply caring yet competitive relationship with my oldest friend and fellow writer, Grant Gerald Miller, I'm not sure where I'd be right now. Grant, we are in this thing together, and I am a better man knowing you are there.

I began writing this book in 2008. My first publication was part of a handsome hand-bound letterpress journal called *Pig*. I'd like to thank Jennifer Callahan, the artist and editor responsible for this important milestone. I'd also like to thank Bret Lott at *Crazyhorse* for publishing "Rain over Memphis," Ashley Rivers at *Redivider* for "Thirteenth Street and Failing," Jullianne Ballou and Caitlin Love at *Oxford American* for "Arrow of Light," Dan Sheehan at *Guernica* for working with me on "The Junk Trade," Kat Moore at the *Pinch* for "Superman Dam Fool," Terry Kennedy at *storySouth* for "Dear Brother," Steven Leyva at *Little Patuxent Review* for "Rock and Roll High School," and David Lazar and Jenn Tatum at *Hotel Amerika* for "Barking Hours."

Thank you, Memphis folks, for inspiring me when I was very young.

Thank you, Olympia folks, for challenging me to interact with the world in more compassionate and radical ways.

I am very happy that *Meander Belt* found a home with University of Nebraska's American Lives Series and I would like to thank Erin Cuddy, Haley Mendlik, Nathan Putens, Anna Weir, Emily Wendell, and Tobias Wolff for all of their hard work.

Finally, I would like to thank the following writers and mentors for all their generosity, advice, support, and friendship: Catina Bacote, Jullianne Ballou, Eli Berkowitz, Amy Bernhard, Rick Chess, Bill Clegg for his kindness, Bernard Cooper, John D'Agata, Antonio Del Toro, Juliet Escoria, Patricia Foster, Jonathan Gharraie, Vivian Gornick, Stephanie Elizondo Griest, Andy Grim, Robin Hemley, Lori Horvitz, Nazli Inal, Adam Jernigan, Elliott Krause, Caitlin Love, Mamone and Queer Appalachia, Tammy Martin, Scott McClanahan, Jim McKean, Katherine Min, Lucy Morris, Howard Parsons and Travelin' Appalachians Revue, Jeff Porter, Gillian Wiley Rose, Helen Rubenstein, Parker Stomach, Jessie van Eerden, Daniel Wallace, Justin Wymer, Larry Ypil, and more I'm sure that I am leaving out.

What Becomes You
by Aaron Raz Link and Hilda Raz

*Queen of the Fall: A Memoir
of Girls and Goddesses*
by Sonja Livingston

*The Virgin of Prince Street:
Expeditions into Devotion*
by Sonja Livingston

Such a Life
by Lee Martin

Turning Bones
by Lee Martin

In Rooms of Memory: Essays
by Hilary Masters

Island in the City: A Memoir
by Micah McCrary

Between Panic and Desire
by Dinty W. Moore

*Meander Belt: Family, Loss,
and Coming of Age in the
Working-Class South*
by M. Randal O'Wain

Sleep in Me
by Jon Pineda

*The Solace of Stones: Finding
a Way through Wilderness*
by Julie Riddle

*Works Cited: An Alphabetical Odyssey
of Mayhem and Misbehavior*
by Brandon R. Schrand

Thoughts from a Queen-Sized Bed
by Mimi Schwartz

*My Ruby Slippers:
The Road Back to Kansas*
by Tracy Seeley

The Fortune Teller's Kiss
by Brenda Serotte

Gang of One: Memoirs of a Red Guard
by Fan Shen

Just Breathe Normally
by Peggy Shumaker

*The Pat Boone Fan Club: My Life
as a White Anglo-Saxon Jew*
by Sue William Silverman

Scraping By in the Big Eighties
by Natalia Rachel Singer

In the Shadow of Memory
by Floyd Skloot

*Secret Frequencies: A New
York Education*
by John Skoyles

The Days Are Gods
by Liz Stephens

Phantom Limb
by Janet Sternburg

*When We Were Ghouls:
A Memoir of Ghost Stories*
by Amy E. Wallen

*Yellowstone Autumn: A Season of
Discovery in a Wondrous Land*
by W. D. Wetherell

This Fish Is Fowl: Essays of Being
by Xu Xi

To order or obtain more information on these or other University
of Nebraska Press titles, visit nebraskapress.unl.edu.